The Motorcycle Safety Foundation's Guide To

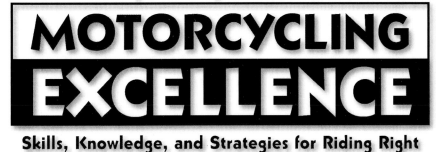

MOTORCYCLING EXCELLENCE

Skills, Knowledge, and Strategies for Riding Right

The More You Know, The Better It Gets

A Whirlaway Book
Whitehorse Press
North Conway, New Hampshire

Cover illustration by Hector Cademartori

Edited by Nate Rauba, with additional editing by Peter Fassnacht, Julie Filatoff, and Gerald Lotto.

We recognize that some words, model names and designations mentioned herein are the property of the trademark holder. We use them for identification purposes only.

The rider in a triangle is a registered trademark of the Motorcycle Safety Foundation.

The names Whirlaway and Whitehorse Press are trademarks of Kennedy Associates.

Whitehorse Press books are also available at discounts in bulk quantity for sales and promotional use. For details about special sales or for a catalog of motorcycling books and videos, write to the Publisher:

Whitehorse Press
P.O. Box 60
North Conway, New Hampshire 03860-0060

ISBN 1-884313-01-9

10   9   8   7   6

Printed in the United States of America

This book is dedicated to everyone who
continually strives to be a better motorcyclist.

Notice

The information contained in this publication is offered for the benefit of those who have an interest in riding motorcycles. The information has been compiled from publications, interviews, and observations of individuals and organizations familiar with the use of motorcycles and training. Because there are many differences in product design, riding styles, Federal, State, and local laws, there may be organizations and individuals who hold differing opinions. Consult your local regulatory agencies for information concerning the operation of motorcycles in your area. Although the Motorcycle Safety Foundation will continue to research, field test, and publish responsible viewpoints on the subject, MSF and the publisher disclaim any liability for the views expressed herein.

Acknowledgements

The Motorcycle Safety Foundation wishes to thank the many dedicated people who work together to improve the safety of motorcyclists on the nation's streets and highways. This includes MSF-certified *RiderCourse* Instructors and Chief Instructors; Motorcyclist-Licensing Examiners; and Administrators and Coordinators of all kinds.

We sincerely appreciate the assistance of all who made this book a reality, including:

AGV USA Corp.

Bill Berroth of Acerbis USA

Hector Cademartori

Rich Chenet

Joe Colombero and Mike Webb of American Suzuki

Rich Cox of Slide Action

Scott Dewey of Fox Racing

Robert Enriquez of Robert Enriquez Illustration

Sukoshi Fahey of Pirelli Motorcycle Tire Div.

Patty Hentges of Intersport Fashions West

Daniel Kennedy and the staff of Whitehorse Press

Gerald Lotto of the Massachusetts Motorcycle Rider Education Program

JoAnne Meeker of The Creative Line

Rick Mitchell of American Honda Motor Co., Inc.

Bruce Porter and Brian Weston of Arai Helmet Ltd.

J.T. Smith of JTS Consulting

Joel Smith of Glen Helen Off-Highway Vehicle Park

and the staff of the Motorcycle Safety Foundation.

The Motorcycle Safety Foundation would especially like to thank its Board of Trustees, comprised of staff members from: American Honda Motor Co., Inc.; American Suzuki Motor Corp.; Kawasaki Motors Corporation, USA; Yamaha Motor Corporation, USA; and BMW of North America, Inc.

Contents

Introduction

Who Is the Motorcycle Safety Foundation?

Since March 1973, the Motorcycle Safety Foundation (MSF) has set internationally recognized standards of excellence in motorcycle safety. The MSF's purpose is to improve the safety of motorcyclists on the nation's streets and highways. Our programs focus on the motorcycle operator, like you. We do not deal with design or manufacture. Specifically, we:

- make high-quality motorcycle rider-education courses available for new and experienced riders (over 1.2 million riders have been trained);
- encourage and assist states in adopting effective motorcycle-operator licensing practices;
- expand the collection of data and information on motorcycle safety;
- inform the public about the safety practices and responsibilities of both motorcyclists and car drivers; and
- represent motorcycle-safety interests to state and federal governments.

The MSF works with the National Highway Traffic Safety Administration, state governments, and other organizations—like the National Association of State Motorcycle Safety Administrators.

The Motorcycle Safety Foundation is a national, nonprofit organization sponsored by the U.S. distributors of Honda, Suzuki, Kawasaki, Yamaha, and BMW motorcycles.

Why This Book?

Riding a motorcycle can be a challenge! To ride a motorcycle safely, you need skill and knowledge. But how do you get that skill and knowledge?

The best way is to take a course specifically designed to teach you the mental and physical skills needed to control your motorcycle, and the knowledge to apply those skills appropriately. We recommend taking an MSF *RiderCourse*—like the *Motorcycle RiderCourse: Riding and Street Skills* if you're a beginning rider, or the *Experienced RiderCourse* if you have been riding for some time. Bettering your skills through training and practice will increase your riding enjoyment and decrease your chance of a mishap.

Until you take a course—or to add to the knowledge you learn in a hands-on environment—you can read this book. Although it can't take the place of learning from a certified motorcycle-safety instructor, it's filled with information to help you increase your skill and knowledge when riding a motorcycle.

The book is divided into four parts. First is "On Your Mark: Preparing Yourself And Your Bike." We'll discuss both the mental and physical preparation necessary before you even swing a leg over the seat. Second is "Get Set: Street Strategies For Smart Riders." Although traffic conditions are continually changing, by learning and applying street strategies you can anticipate where problems may crop up. Third is "Go: Advanced Theory For Experienced Riders." Here you'll find technical information about traction, countersteering, cornering, and turning. Finally, in "You're On Your Way," we'll touch briefly on off-highway riding, and what to do now that you've read *Motorcycling Excellence*.

If you're reading this book, you're already intrigued by two-wheeled transportation. But we bet you'll be surprised at all the different answers to our first question: Why do people ride?

PART I

The Challenge of Motorcycling

1

Why Do People Ride?

Why do people ride motorcycles? There are probably as many reasons as there are motorcyclists. If you commute, think about how much more you like the ride to and from work than your actual job! If you tour, you're probably already planning the next trip before you even return from the one you're on. If you're a sport rider, the wait for Sunday morning and that ride in the twisties is almost more than you can bear. If you're a racer, there's no substitute for the adrenaline rush you can only get in racetrack or off-road competition. Perhaps the most common reason is that riding a motorcycle is just plain fun! When you ride you're out in the open, a part of the environment. You are not in a confined space, so there's a tremendous sense of freedom.

Besides the pure joy of motorcycling, other reasons riders may cite are:

- motorcycles get good fuel mileage
- motorcycles are easy to park
- riding is something they've always wanted to do
- it makes commuting more fun and easier
- it's challenging
- motorcycles can be inexpensive to purchase and operate
- the camaraderie among riders
- sharing the riding experience with someone close.

Whatever the reasons, the first step to enjoying motorcycles is understanding a little about them.

It's plain to see that a motorcycle is much different than a car. Of course, cars are bigger and have two more wheels. They enclose the occupant in a steel compartment. Let's look at what this means to the motorcyclist.

Motorcycles are smaller and easier to park. They can carry only one passenger and not much luggage. And because motorcycles are smaller and have fewer lights, they are often more difficult to see in traffic.

Motorcycles are lightweight. You can make them respond quickly to your control. But motorcycles can be sensitive to other forces such as wind and road surfaces.

Motorcycles are more maneuverable at low speeds. A skilled, experienced rider can swerve and stop a motorcycle in less space than a car would use.

Motorcycles provide less protection. The rider is more exposed to the environment, including wind, rain, sun, bugs, and traffic, to name a few.

Motorcycles must be balanced when stopped or moving slowly. A motorcycle cannot stand up by itself. It needs your help and attention.

The most critical differences between cars and motorcycles are stability and vulnerability.

What this all means is that you operate a motorcycle differently than you drive an automobile.

The Challenge of Motorcycling

Motorcycling is a challenge. It is best met with sharply honed physical skills and finely tuned mental processes. It also has an element of risk. But that risk can be minimized by being a responsible, skilled rider. (That's you!)

What Research Shows

Studies have pointed out some predictable, and some surprising, conclusions about motorcycle safety.

A motorcycle rider is physically vulnerable. In a crash, a rider and passenger are more likely to be injured than an automobile driver and passenger. Injuries, however, can be reduced by riders and passengers wearing reasonable protective gear.

A motorcycle rider's judgment is critical. In single-vehicle crashes, rider error is the most common cause. Crashes with other vehicles also occur because either one or both operators make errors in judgment. Many collisions and injuries could have been avoided if the motorcycle rider had known when and how to swerve or brake.

The ability to see the motorcycle is critical. Automobile drivers often misjudge the approach speed and distance of a motorcycle. Some completely fail to notice a motorcycle prior to impact. The more visible a motorcyclist is, the less chance of accident involvement.

It might seem that research studies paint a bleak picture of motorcycling. But consider that riders who were self-taught or who learned from family or friends were about twice as likely to be involved in accidents. More than 40% of those accident-involved riders lacked the proper motorcycle license endorsement.

Rider education goes beyond basic skills. Rider education, like pilot training, gives you the experience to correctly deal with the unexpected situation that you hope never happens. By reading this book, you are beginning—or furthering—your "pilot training."

How to Meet the Challenge of Motorcycling

Manage Risk

Is it possible to ride a motorcycle safely? Technically you can't, if you consider the dictionary's definition of "safe" as an absence of risk—in fact, there are few things that don't involve risk. Since you can't ride completely without risk, you must manage time and space to recognize and deal with hazards, reducing risk as much as practical. To successfully manage and reduce risk you should have a good understanding of the characteristics of risk.

Risk is defined as "the chance or probability of injury, damage, or loss." When you ride, or do anything, for that matter, *some level of risk always exists.* There is *always* a chance of an undesired and harmful event occurring, and the probability of that event is constantly changing. The probability can increase or decrease rapidly as elements move through time and space. When a hazard goes undetected, risk increases. Suddenly—and unexpectedly—you could be in a trap!

Most of the time there is a difference between your perception of risk and the actual level of risk present. In activities such as hang gliding, deep-sea diving or sky diving, the relative level of risk is quite apparent. The traffic environment is one people are accustomed to; they face risks frequently. It's a situation in which you can easily become complacent about the obvious risks present.

You can analyze, contrast, and compare risk to determine its relative degree. To do this, you assess a situation and, on a comparative basis, determine both the worst and the best possible outcomes. Ask yourself how you would respond if a certain set of circumstances came together. This analysis should be done with the individual hazards, by priority, as well as the effects of all possible events. Mentally build a worst-case scenario for the perceived hazards and think about what you would do to lessen their effects.

Riding is an activity in which you can change your risk level. You can substantially increase or decrease the amount of risk present by your riding actions. If you couldn't do this, you would just aim your motorcycle down the highway and put yourself totally in the hands of fate.

When you ride, you force other road users to accept risks that result from *your* riding behavior. At the same time, you must also share the risk resulting from *their* behavior. Constantly being aware of this relationship helps you control risk. You must try to manage situations where the shared risks are uncomfortable. Understanding shared risk also helps you to not force a risk level on others that they may not want.

Preparation, knowledge, and responsibility are the keys to meeting motorcycling's challenge and minimizing risk.

Prepare to Ride

Ensuring that your motorcycle is mechanically ready is a part of preparation. Selecting the right protective gear to wear is also part of preparation. But don't overlook *yourself*. Your physical and mental preparation are as important as correct tire pressures and a good helmet.

And you aren't completely prepared to ride until you've been properly licensed by your state motor-vehicle agency (see Appendix B).

Understand Your Abilities

To ride safely, you must know the limits of your abilities—what you can do, what you know. You must also know the capabilities of your motorcycle—how it performs in a curve, how quickly it can stop. And you must understand the environment in which you are riding—such as the road surface, visibility, traffic laws and the flow of traffic.

Accept Your Responsibilities

Once you are prepared, once you know the limits of your environment and your motorcycle, and once you understand the limits of your abilities, you must take responsibility for operating within those limits.

Consider Joe Motorcyclist, riding down a two-lane road. Joe is a courteous rider. He waves to other riders. He's the kind of guy who would stop to help another motorcyclist who is stranded on the road.

A car turns left in front of Joe at an intersection. Joe is surprised and overreacts. He inadvertently applies too much pressure to the rear brake pedal and fails to use the front brake at all. He locks up the rear brakes and slides into the car. In the collision, Joe is injured.

Does all the blame for Joe's injury rest with the driver of the car? After all, the driver was legally wrong when he failed to yield. How does Joe share the blame? He was not maintaining adequate visual lead, failed to properly perform maximum braking, and was relying on the judgment of the car driver.

Not only that, who had the most to lose? Joe. Why? Because he had the greater chance of personal injury.

Someone once stated this philosophy about riding:

"When I ride, I like surprises I can smile about. I'm riding down that road and see that car that could pull out in front of me. I prepare by slowing down, maybe changing lane position, and preparing to brake harder, if necessary. But the car *doesn't* pull out. That's a surprise I can smile about.

"Or how about: It's nighttime. I see two small green spheres reflecting in the trees to the side of the road. I slow down, cover the brakes, and increase scanning, rapidly searching the area. I am careful not to focus on a single point. Moments later, I realize I was correct—it's a deer along the side of the road that didn't jump out. It's another surprise I can smile about!

"As a motorcyclist, I trust my judgment. If at all possible, I also try not to place my future in the trust of *another* person's judgment. I don't trust that the car driver will not pull out in front of me.

"I take responsibility for what happens to me."

Self-Test for Chapter 1:
The Challenge of Motorcycling

Choose the best answer for each question.

1. What is one of the best ways to obtain the skill and knowledge necessary to ride a motorcycle safely?

   a. Get tips from a friend who rides.
   b. Hire a professional racer to teach you.
   c. Complete a *Motorcycle RiderCourse*.
   d. Read motorcycle magazines.

2. What is the most common cause of single-vehicle motorcycle crashes?

   a. Inattention.
   b. Rider error.
   c. Flat tire.
   d. Oil spot on the road.

3. Which of the following *won't* help you to minimize risk?

   a. Knowledge.
   b. Responsibility.
   c. Preparation.
   d. Determination.

4. Which of the following items is the most essential to have when you ride on the street?

   a. A *Motorcycle RiderCourse* graduate card.
   b. A full gas tank.
   c. Bungee cords.
   d. A proper license or endorsement.

   (Answers appear on page 176.)

Buying Your First Motorcycle . . .

Choosing the Right Ride

You're thinking about buying your first bike and walk into your local motorcycle dealer. Several different models are displayed, and each one looks different from the others. There are big ones, small ones, racy-looking models shrouded in plastic, others with no bodywork at all, and even one with a trunk! To the uninitiated, this array of motorcycles may be intimidating.

How do you choose the right one to buy?

There are several different forms of riding, each with its distinct characteristics. There are twisty mountain roads to be explored, or perhaps you intend to mainly cruise around town. Many riders use motorcycles for their daily commute to work. Some love getting out on the highway for a long-distance weekend adventure.

Choosing a particular type of bike can be a little confusing at first. They each work best for different things. You must decide on the style of ride you want and carefully choose the features you will use. That's when you're ready to do some serious shopping.

Choosing a motorcycle involves matching your needs and your favorite style of riding with the types and sizes offered. Let's take a closer look at some of the popular styles of motorcycles available and what they have to offer.

First there is the **standard,** general-purpose motorcycle. This type of bike has a comfortable balance between performance and style. Some lean to the sporting side, others to touring. But all

The standard, general-purpose motorcycle is ideal for getting your start in motorcycling.

"standards" have one thing in common: they're ideal for getting your start in motorcycling.

Standard bikes are characterized by a classic upright riding position with plenty of room for a passenger. They typically come from the manufacturer with very little or no bodywork. Their engines aren't hidden behind plastic panels, so it's easier for the owner to perform regularly scheduled maintenance. You can choose from several models, in all engine sizes, to meet your riding needs, budget, and experience.

The manufacturers, and many aftermarket companies, offer a variety of accessories for the standard-style motorcycle. Accessories like fairings, windshields, luggage racks, and saddlebags will help you on a long ride, or add that personal touch to your motorcycle.

(continued)

Cruisers are the factory-built descendants of the classic custom motorcycle.

Touring motorcycles are designed to provide the highest levels of comfort and carrying capacity.

But maybe you want to make a stronger personal statement. Bring on the **cruisers.** Here's a combination of style and performance that's sure to turn heads. As the name implies, cruisers are great for a short hop down the highway or just cruisin' the boulevard. And many are the factory-built descendants of the classic custom. You get a distinctive look and feel, backed by solid engineering and the reliability you'd expect from a modern motorcycle.

There are several engine types and power levels to choose from. With plenty of gleaming chrome and paint that looks like it's straight from the custom shop, you'll be ready to move out in style. Cruisers also offer a laid-back ride that's great for sharing with a special friend.

Say you dream of the great adventure. The open roads beckon. You know there's only one way to see the world and that's up close and personal. You'll probably want to pack more than just your toothbrush. Enter the grand **touring** motorcycle.

These are motorcycles built to take you there—and back. Like the others, they do so many things very well. But these bikes were clearly designed with one thing in mind: to provide the rider and passenger with the highest levels of comfort and carrying capacity for long-distance rides.

Aerodynamically engineered fairings and windshields surround the rider for comfort and protection from wind and inclement weather. Large-capacity luggage compartments hold the personal things that make a weekend or a week-long ride civilized. Generous gas-tank capacities permit longer ranges between stops.

The touring models have powerful, reliable engines that match their load capabilities. You'll find a wide variety of features that cater to the riders' needs, like state-of-the-art stereos, CBs and rider/passenger intercoms, cruise control, and plush adjustable suspension.

(continued)

Scooters have step-through frames and automatic transmissions.

Sportbikes capture the spirit of their all-out competition cousins.

Perhaps you'd rather stay a little closer to home. For the commute to school and work or running errands, **scooters** provide another stylish form of motorcycling. Scooters are characterized by their distinctly styled, step-through frame and automatic transmissions. They're lightweight, fuel efficient, and easy to own and operate. Many have special storage spaces and all the standard features you would expect of motorcycles.

For some, motorcycling is a single-minded pursuit. For them the technological prowess of today's **sportbikes** is what it's all about. These motorcycles embody the latest in performance technology and design. They capture the spirit of their all-out competition cousins in their style and hardware. And they make carving through a curving mountain road a joy.

Sportbikes bristle with the latest in brake, tire, and suspension components. Their engines come in every capacity, with a high-specific output. These motorcycles are easily recognizable by their sleek aerodynamic bodywork and a riding position that puts the rider closely in tune with every movement on the road. State-of-the-art in two-wheel technology doesn't get any better!

Some riders may find the sportbikes' hunched-over, competition-style riding position to be too uncomfortable for long-range touring rides. But they want comfort and reasonable performance.

(continued)

Sport-touring motorcycles are a cross between a grand-touring rig and a sportbike.

Dual-purpose motorcycles are street-legal, yet can be ridden off the highway.

The **sport-touring** class meets their demands. These motorcycles are a cross between the grand-touring rig and a sportbike. The sport tourer has the sleek bodywork of a sportbike, yet the rider sits in a more traditional, upright position and is often shielded by a windscreen. Detachable saddlebags can be installed for a multi-day journey, or removed when there is no need to carry luggage. They are much lighter than traditional touring bikes so that less effort is required for maneuvering on twisty roads.

Motorcycling is about adventure, and for some riders staying on the highways is just too restrictive. There's a whole world of back roads, Forest Service access roads and even trails that just have to be explored. **Dual-purpose** motorcycles, also commonly known as dual-sport, were designed to meet this need.

These bikes feature all the equipment needed to be street-legal, like lights, mirrors, turn signals, and clean, quiet exhaust systems. And they're also lightweight, rugged and feature suspension and engine characteristics that let you take on the challenges of the off-highway world. Because of their simple, rugged, lightweight designs, they make great do-everything, first-time motorcycles, and at affordable prices, too.

(Continued)

. . . Buying Your First Motorcycle

Now that you know what types of motorcycles are available, you can decide exactly what type will fill your needs. Many options may be available on any given model, too. When you are ready to buy, visit several dealers in your area. Find one whose staff is knowledgeable and friendly. Try several models until you find one that feels right. Don't be afraid to ask questions. Most motorcycle salespeople are eager to help share the joy of motorcycling.

When you do purchase your new motorcycle, be sure to get the proper motorcycle-operator endorsement on your driver's license. Obtain the proper insurance coverage. It's also a good idea to take a *Motorcycle RiderCourse* on your new motorcycle so that you will be familiar with how it responds to your skills.

To learn more about buying a motorcycle, preparing to ride, how to finance, and how to get insured, get the *Straight Facts* brochures from your dealer, or call Discover Today's Motorcycling at 1-800-833-3995. ∎

Let's begin with the basic skills you need to ride a motorcycle. As you would imagine, there's more to it than sitting down, turning the throttle, and riding away.

Reading this chapter will not teach you how to ride; only practice will do that. It will, however, outline those basic skills.

Mounting the Motorcycle

Always mount from the left side. Hold both handgrips and squeeze the front brake with your right hand to prevent the motorcycle from rolling. Swing your right leg over the seat. Straighten up the bike. Sit on the seat and raise the sidestand with your foot (or push off the centerstand). Adjust the mirrors so that you see just a small portion of your shoulders in the reflection.

Starting the Engine

Use FINE-C as a pre-start checklist:

- **Fuel** – Fuel valve on. (Some motorcycles do not have a manual fuel valve.)
- **Ignition** – Ignition switch on.
- **Neutral** – Shift the transmission to neutral. Check the neutral light and roll the motorcycle to be sure that it's not in gear.
- **Engine cut-off switch** – Set the switch to the run position.

- **Choke & clutch** – Set the choke, if necessary, according to the engine's temperature. Squeezing the clutch is a good idea when starting your motorcycle, and may be required on some models.

To start the engine with an electric starter, merely press the starter button. To kickstart the motorcycle, lean the bike slightly to the left and fold out the kick starter. Place the ball of your foot on the lever. With a cold engine, keep the throttle closed. A warm engine may require a slightly open throttle. Kick the lever straight down with a quick motion and don't let your foot slip off at the bottom. Repeat the process as necessary. Fold the kick starter back in before riding.

Using the Friction Zone to Get the Motorcycle Underway

The friction zone is that area of clutch-lever travel where the clutch just starts to transmit power to the rear wheel. Here's how to find the friction zone: Squeeze the clutch. Shift to first gear. Place both feet on the ground. Hold the throttle slightly open and *slowly* ease the clutch lever out until the engine starts to slow down and the bike starts to move forward. This is called the "friction zone." Squeeze in the clutch lever and practice the technique again.

The engine may stall if you do not open the throttle enough or if you release the clutch too quickly. If you feel the engine stalling, squeeze

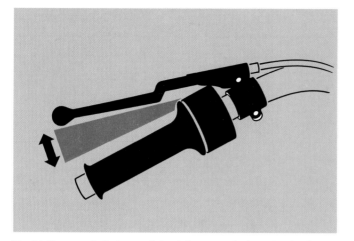

The friction zone is that area of clutch-lever travel where the clutch just starts to transmit power to the rear wheel, as shown by the red triangle.

Good posture—back straight, head and eyes up—will make you comfortable on your bike and improve your riding.

in the clutch lever, release the throttle, and try again.

Riding Posture

Good posture will make you comfortable on the motorcycle and improve your riding.

Sit with your back straight and your head and eyes up. Place both feet on the pegs as the motorcycle begins to move. Keep your knees and elbows in and cover the rear brake and shift lever with your feet. Hold the handgrips with your right wrist down and the knuckles up. Cover the clutch with all four fingers. Sit far enough forward so your elbows are slightly bent and, above all, relax!

Turning

There are four key steps to turning:

- SLOW
- LOOK
- LEAN
- ROLL

Slow

Reduce speed before the turn by closing the throttle, downshifting, and, if necessary, applying both brakes.

Look

Use your head and eyes for directional control. Look through the turn to where you want to go. Turn your head, not your shoulders or just your eyes.

Lean

To turn, the motorcycle must lean. To lean the motorcycle, press on the handgrip in the direction of the turn. Press left—lean left—go left. Press right—lean right—go right. (This may seem contrary to what you would think; see Chapter 13 for more information.) Higher speeds and/or tighter turns require more lean.

In normal turns, the rider and the motorcycle should lean together. You and the motorcycle should become one. In slow, tight turns, lean the motorcycle only and keep your body straight.

Roll

Roll on the throttle through the turn. Maintain steady speed or gently accelerate. Avoid deceleration or rapid acceleration while in the turn.

Shifting

You should change gears to keep the engine speed within its best operating range as the motorcycle speed changes. Use lower gears for lower speeds and higher gears for higher speeds.

Upshift

Upshift when increasing speed. First, roll off the throttle as you squeeze the clutch. When the throttle is closed and the clutch fully disengaged, lift the shift lever firmly and positively until it stops. Then smoothly ease out the clutch as you roll on the throttle.

Upshift soon enough to prevent over-revving the engine, but not so soon as to cause lugging.

Downshift

Downshift when decreasing speed. Remember, just selecting a lower gear and quickly releasing the clutch has a similar effect to stepping hard on the rear brake! Roll off the throttle as you squeeze the clutch. Press down on the shift lever firmly. Then slightly roll on the throttle as you smoothly ease out the clutch. Be sure that the motorcycle's speed is low enough for the next lower gear to prevent over-revving the engine, but shift down soon enough to prevent lugging the engine.

To use engine braking, shift down one gear at a time and release the clutch after each downshift. When coming to a stop, you may want to avoid engine braking by downshifting to first gear without releasing the clutch between downshifts.

When turning, look through the turn in the direction you want to go. Turn your head, not your shoulders or just your eyes.

Stopping

To stop, your hands and feet work together—in and down at the same time. Squeeze the clutch and the front brake as you press on the brake pedal and downshift to first gear. Be sure to keep that clutch disengaged!

Always use both brakes to stop. The front brake can provide 70% or more of the stopping power. Some motorcycles have integrated braking systems that link the front and rear brakes together on application of the brake pedal, and some are even equipped with anti-lock braking systems.

Over-revving the engine when stopping can be caused by not releasing the throttle while squeezing the brake. Lugging and stalling the engine can be caused by not squeezing the clutch.

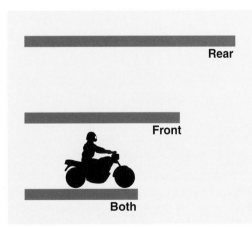

Always use both brakes together. You'll stop in the shortest distance.

Skidding can be caused by overuse of the rear brake.

Stopping The Engine

Turn the engine cut-off switch to OFF. Make this a habit so you can reach the switch quickly if you need to. Turn off the ignition switch and the fuel valve (if your motorcycle has one).

Dismounting The Motorcycle

Make sure you are in first gear. Squeeze the front brake as you lower the sidestand with your foot.

Lean the motorcycle left on the sidestand and swing your right leg over the seat. Turn the handlebars toward the sidestand for more stability, and lock the forks.

What we've outlined here are the very basics for riding a motorcycle. Every motorcycle is different. Out on the road things become much more complex. You must coordinate all of these basics along with gathering information about your riding environment. Before each ride, you should prepare for the challenges that lie ahead.

Self-Test for Chapter 2: Basic Riding Skills

Choose the best answer for each question.

1. From which side should you mount a motorcycle?

    a. Left.
    b. Right.
    c. Front.
    d. Rear.

2. What is the "friction zone"?

    a. Where the tires meet the road.
    b. An unlubricated engine part.
    c. Where the clutch just starts to transmit power to the rear wheel.
    d. Brake pads.

3. Name the four steps to turning a motorcycle.

    _____

    _____

    _____

    _____

4. How much of the brakes' stopping power does the front brake normally provide?

    a. 50%
    b. 100%
    c. 25%
    d. 70%

    (Answers appear on page 176.)

Motorcycle Controls

Part of the joy of motorcycling is having your bike perform as if it were an extension of your body. To accomplish this, the first thing you need to know is what controls you use to ride a motorcycle and how you operate them.

Primary Controls

Use both hands and both feet to operate the five major controls that make a motorcycle go and stop:
– Throttle
– Clutch lever
– Gear-shift lever
– Front brake lever
– Rear brake lever

1. Throttle – Controls engine speed. Roll "on" toward rider and "off" away from rider. Springs back to idle position.

2. Clutch – Connects power from the engine to the rear wheel. Squeeze to disengage. Ease slowly to engage.

3. Gear shift – Lift lever to upshift one gear at a time. Press down to downshift one gear at a time. Typical pattern: 1-N-2-3-4-5-(6).

4. Front brake – Squeeze to operate.

5. Rear brake – Press down to operate.

Other Controls And Equipment

6. Fuel-supply valve – Controls fuel supply to engine. Turn to ON, OFF, RESERVE, or PRIME.

7. Ignition – Key selects ON, OFF, PARK, or LOCK.

8. Choke – On for cold starts.

9. Engine cut-off switch – Shuts off engine.

10. Electric starter – Push to start engine.

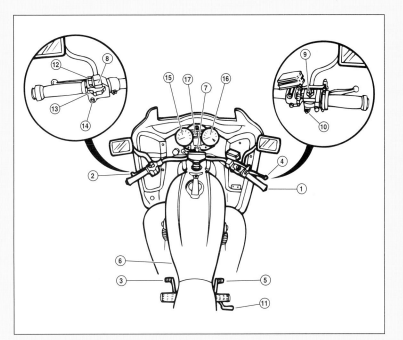

Motorcycle Controls

11. Kick starter – Thrust down with foot to start engine.

12. Headlight beam – Selects low or high beam.

13. Turn signals – Usually do not cancel automatically.

14. Horn – Press to operate.

15. Speedometer – Includes an odometer to show total miles ridden.

16. Tachometer – Indicates engine speed. Never run the engine at an rpm indicated by the red zone.

17. Indicator lights – Indicates neutral, high beam, turn signals, and other conditions such as: engine-oil pressure, sidestand down, etc.

18. Side & centerstands – Support the motorcycle when parked.

Refer to your owner's manual for a detailed description of your particular bike. ∎

Scooters Are Motorcycles, Too . . .

Do you think that because a scooter is different that it's not a motorcycle? Think again.

Scooters are indeed considered motorcycles. They're just a different style, and have their own unique characteristics.

Besides being smaller, one of the most obvious differences is that a scooter doesn't have a traditional motorcycle frame. Where you normally see a fuel tank, there is nothing but air. This makes it easy to mount a scooter. You can still swing your leg over the seat, but most riders prefer to simply "step through" then sit on the seat. Whatever method you use, just make sure you squeeze the front brake so the machine doesn't roll out from under you.

Since there's no gas tank for scooter riders to put their knees against, they should tuck them in comfortably within the limits of the fairing or floorboard.

Riding a scooter can be quite a different experience than riding a motorcycle. Scooters are commonly equipped with an automatic clutch that engages the transmission gears at a pre-set engine speed above normal idle. When moving slowly, the clutch becomes disengaged and no power is transmitted to the rear wheel. This also creates a lag between rolling on the throttle and when power actually gets to the rear wheel.

(continued)

A scooter generally responds more quickly to steering input because of smaller-diameter wheels, shorter wheelbase, lower center of gravity, and steeper steering angle.

. . . Scooters Are Motorcycles, Too

"Revving" the engine activates the automatic clutch. So always be sure the scooter is restrained by the brakes or (when parked on its centerstand) that the parking brake lock is set. A spinning rear wheel that suddenly contacts the ground could cause an accident. Ease off the brakes slowly and roll on the throttle to move forward.

Once underway, there is no need to shift, since scooters have automatic transmissions.

Stopping a scooter can be much the same as braking a regular motorcycle. Some models have both brakes operated by hand, with the left side activating the rear brake. Other scooters have a traditional rear brake activated by the right foot.

Whatever the configuration, scooter riders should learn and practice maximum braking techniques. Weight shifts forward under braking, and this can create a unique problem for scooter riders who don't use the proper riding posture. Many scooter riders tend to ride with their left foot placed well back on the floorboard. This can create a problem under hard braking. As weight shifts forward, riders in this position are likely to brace themselves with the right foot to prevent sliding forward on the seat. With the left foot back, this increases pressure on the brake pedal and is likely to create overbraking and rear-wheel lockup.

Another difference scooter riders should be aware of is the amount of force necessary to steer (see Chapter 13, Countersteering). Generally, a scooter responds more quickly to a press on the handgrip because it has smaller-diameter wheels, a shorter wheelbase, a lower center of gravity, and a steeper steering angle. Therefore, the press on the grip need not be as strong as the press used to steer a "regular" motorcycle.

Understanding the distinct nature of scooters will help make your ride a more pleasant experience. And just as can be said about riding a regular motorcycle, the more you know, the better it gets. ■

The Un-Rider . . .

About five years ago a dealer asked a customer who had just bought a motorcycle if he could ride.

"Can I ride?" quipped the young Sir Galahad. "Watch this . . ."

With that he promptly wheeled out of the dealer's back lot, across six busy lanes of a downtown street, and launched the motorcycle through the large, plate-glass window of a store across the street. Fortunately, he fell off before flame-out and re-entry.

The proprietors of the store, two elderly ladies, identifying several key characteristics that distinguished the approaching vehicle from a prospective customer, sought refuge in a small washroom. Investigating officers spent some time coaxing them out to give evidence.

Apart from possessing the IQ of a table lamp, the rider had no insurance. And no license.

Would it surprise you to learn that not too long ago, estimates put the proportion of unlicensed motorcyclists in the United States as high as 65%?

"We figure it's down to about 50% these days," says Carl Spurgeon, Director of Licensing for the Motorcycle Safety Foundation. "The trouble is, that's a guess. And it could be anybody's guess. The only time we can pinpoint the figures with any accuracy, usually, is when a rider is involved in an accident."

Such a body count may be one way of doing it, but there are other ways to keep score—a police crackdown, for example.

Because of the high numbers of un-riders (as we call unlicensed motorcyclists) generating sonic shock waves and burnt rubber in the San Fernando Valley of California, the Los Angeles Police Department stepped in. A special detail, empowered to impound the bikes of unlicensed riders, started patrolling the valley in 1987. Their first year of business resulted in 5,000 traffic tickets and 600 motorcycles impounded. In 1988, business picked up. A one-day sweep resulted in 75 traffic citations, five arrests, and 60 motorcycles impounded.

In California, a rider whose bike has been impounded can only get it back by producing a valid motorcycle operator's license and paying hefty towing and storage fees. And in this age of electronic sorcery, computers make it very easy to catch the un-rider.

(continued)

. . . The Un-Rider

Many police agencies—those in Illinois for example—can patch into state Department of Motor Vehicle computers. Just calling in a plate number gives them the registered owner, type of license, endorsements, restrictions, violations, and whether the license is valid or suspended. It may be no coincidence, therefore, that Illinois has one of the lowest unlicensed-rider rates in the country, about 20% at last count.

Some un-riders, who use their bikes once a week for a trip to the beach, may escape the long arm of the law. They may ride intermittently for quite some time before they have an accident or are stopped for a traffic violation and a police officer discovers that they aren't licensed to ride.

But studies show that those un-riders are much more likely to be involved in an accident than legally licensed motorcyclists. Why? According to a California Highway Patrol officer, ". . . the problem is inexperience, poor or no training, and—in some cases—a certain amount of cockiness. A lot of them go into dealerships, buy a motorcycle and go riding without any training whatsoever."

The result, all too often, shows up in accident statistics.

So what's all this got to do with you, the experienced rider who takes fun seriously? Well, at its simplest level, it could mean a bit of inconvenience. Because when police try to crack down on un-riders, they have to use a wide net: a roadside checkpoint at which every motorcyclist must produce a valid license.

But there's much more.

Let's say an unlicensed rider who happens to be insured is involved in an accident. Most state laws require the insurance company to pay the claim, even though the rider shouldn't have been on a motorcycle to begin with. But do you think the company is going to insure this turkey again? And how do you think that company will feel about motorcycle insurance in general as a business proposition?

In addition, insurance rates are based on losses, and if a bunch of inexperienced, untrained un-riders are out there getting into accidents, what do you think that will do to your insurance costs? Have you tried to get reasonable motorcycle insurance lately?

Finally, though, there's an even more ominous concern. If the un-rider keeps showing up in the statistics, expect the big guns to be rolled out. Government will step in. Heavily. And you know what that can mean: over-reaction, over-regulation, and hastily-drafted laws that hurt responsible riders.

So if you're really serious about motorcycling, you need to do something about un-riders. These guys are covering our collective face with egg.

If you know someone who's riding without a license, do that person—and all of us—a favor. Suggest he take a license test. It's not that tough.

And whatever you do, don't lend an un-rider your motorcycle. If a friend tells you he wants to get a taste for riding by sneaking up and down side streets and back alleys on a borrowed bike, why not put in a word for the *Motorcycle RiderCourse: Riding and Street Skills?* (See Chap. 17.)

What better way to introduce anyone to motorcycling? They don't even have to buy a motorcycle—or a helmet. Sure beats breaking store windows . . .   ■

Mental Preparation

3

Riding a motorcycle requires all of your concentration. So the first thing to do is to prepare yourself to process information and respond immediately. Free your mind of distractions that might preoccupy you while riding. Plan your ride before you get on the motorcycle. Consider the types of roads and traffic you may encounter and think about how you might deal with them. And, of course, remember that alcohol and other drugs will dull your thinking and coordination. Avoid them.

Your attitude affects how you perceive situations around you and how you react to others. Stress, anger, grief, and other emotions can all impair your ability to ride. Don't let yourself get into a hazardous situation just because you were unable to pay attention.

Knowledge is another kind of mental preparation. There are several sources of information about your motorcycle and motorcycling in general that will better equip you to ride—like this book, for instance. Publications like motorcycle magazines and safety literature offer you many different perspectives on riding. Your local *RiderCourse* training site is a wonderful resource for a wealth of information.

Know yourself and your limits. For example, you might be riding a new motorcycle for the first time. When is the last time you took a look at your owner's manual? Do you know the machine and its capabilities?

Experience also plays an important role in your perception and judgment. Analyze your riding style, and the situations that you've encountered in the past. Discuss your riding experiences with others and you may find that you have a lot in common!

Some kinds of riding are more demanding than others. Fatigue can become a factor on long tours or late-night rides. Make sure you are in good physical and mental condition and are prepared to meet the challenge of the upcoming ride. Hunger or a need to use rest facilities can take your attention away from the ride. Take care of your physical needs before riding and take frequent rest breaks. Stop, get off your bike, and walk around—ideally, every hour. Limit the distance you ride; about six hours per day is a comfortable limit for most people.

Even age can be considered a form of impairment. Physical reaction time, vision, and other faculties may not be as sprightly as when you were younger. These are limits that must also be taken into consideration as you ride.

Route planning and knowing what the weather holds in store for you affect your physical preparation. It is difficult to be prepared for all contingencies, so knowing the conditions you are likely to encounter will help you to plan effectively. Traffic, construction, and vehicle restrictions all have the potential to impact the time and character of each trip. Consider, too, the importance of protecting yourself from the elements. Changeable weather conditions may require you to adapt your apparel. As the saying goes, "If you don't like the weather, wait five minutes." This is another aspect of motorcycling where the adage, "The More you Know, the Better it Gets," really rings true.

There really isn't a lot to say about mental preparation that isn't covered by common sense. With so little written on the subject, it might be tempting to assume that the topic is unimportant or trivial. Nothing could be further from the truth! Some experts estimate that riding a motorcycle is as much as 90% a mental activity. Certainly, if so much is "riding" on your mental skills and abilities, mental preparation is important topic that deserves your consideration.

Checking Out

Have you ever caught yourself on the road wondering what you were doing for the past couple of minutes? It happens to many of us when we are thinking about something other than the here and now . . . and that's when most accidents happen! In fact, 68% of all accidents occur during the first 12 minutes of a trip, and 57% happen during a trip of less than five miles, when the rider has other things on his or her mind.

Mental preparation is an essential part of managing your risks when riding. Take a few minutes to check your motorcycle and gear before you ride. Even when nothing needs to be adjusted or fixed, the time you spend will help to focus your attention on the ride ahead. ■

Self-Test for Chapter 3:
Mental Preparation

1. How can you prepare yourself mentally for riding?

   a. Free your mind of distractions.

   b. Consider the roads you plan to ride on and the traffic patterns.

   c. Avoid alcohol and other drugs.

   d. All of the above.

2. Ideally, how often should you stop, get off your bike, and walk around?

   a. Every two hours.

   b. Every hour.

   c. When your bike needs gas.

   d. Every 10 minutes.

3. Experts have estimated that riding a motorcycle is as much as _____% a mental activity. (Fill in the blank.)

4. Fatigue and hunger can take your attention away from the mental part of riding, where it belongs. Name two emotions that can also impair your ability to ride.

   _____

   _____

(Answers appear on page 176.)

Riding Straight

4

In the following chapters you'll learn about the skills that enable you to ride more safely. Riding a motorcycle is a demanding and complex task. To become a skilled rider, you must be able to give adequate attention to the riding environment and to the operation of the motorcycle, to identify potential hazards, to make good judgments, and to execute each decision quickly and skillfully. Your ability to perform at your best and to respond to changing road and traffic conditions is influenced by how fit and alert you are.

Alcohol and other drugs, more than any other factor, degrade your ability to think clearly and to ride safely. This chapter examines the risks involved in riding after drinking and how you can intervene to protect yourself and your fellow riders.

Why This Information Is Important

Alcohol is a major contributor to motorcycle accidents, particularly fatal accidents. Data shows that *almost 50%* of all riders killed in motorcycle accidents had been drinking. Only one-third of these riders had a blood-alcohol concentration above the legal limits. The rest had only a few drinks in their systems—enough to impair their riding skills.

The drinking problem is just as extensive among accident-involved motorcyclists as it is among accident-involved automobile drivers. However, motorcyclists are far more likely to be killed or severely injured in an accident. Injuries occur in *90%* of alcohol-involved motorcycle accidents and only 33% of automobile accidents. On a yearly basis, 2,500 motorcyclists are killed and about 50,000 seriously injured in accidents involving alcohol. These statistics are too overwhelming to ignore.

Many people would *never,* under any circumstances, ride a motorcycle after drinking alcohol. Others are willing to take their chances, even though it means the odds are against them. The most effective way to improve *your* chances of riding safely is to become knowledgeable about the effects of alcohol and other drugs. There are positive steps you can take to protect yourself and to prevent others from injuring themselves.

Alcohol enters the bloodstream quickly. Unlike most foods and beverages, it does not need to be digested. Within minutes after being con-

Your body is able to eliminate alcohol at the rate of almost one drink per hour. There is no way to speed up that process, not even drinking coffee.

A 12-ounce can of beer, a 5-ounce glass of wine, or a shot of liquor all contain the same amount of alcohol.

The typical drink contains $\frac{6}{10}$ of an ounce of alcohol. A 12-ounce can of beer, a 5-ounce glass of wine, or a shot of liquor all contain the same amount of alcohol. BAC is determined in part by how much alcohol is consumed.

But there are other factors that contribute to the way alcohol affects people. Gender, physical condition, and food intake are just a few factors that may cause your BAC level to be even higher. The full effects of these factors are not completely known. Alcohol may still accumulate in your body even if you are drinking at a rate of one drink per hour. Abilities and judgment can be affected by that one drink.

The faster you drink, the more alcohol accumulates in your body. The body can only burn off the alcohol in one drink in an hour. Thus, if you consume two drinks in one hour, at the end of that hour, one drink will be burned off and one will remain in your bloodstream.

To figure out how many drinks are in the bloodstream, use the formula below:

drinks consumed – hours = drinks left

Weight is also a factor in determining BAC. A larger person will not accumulate as high a concentration of alcohol for each drink consumed. This is because they have more blood and other bodily fluids and BAC is the percentage of alcohol *in relation to* other fluids in the body.

For example, people who are small in stature and weigh less than 120 pounds (54 kg) will generally become intoxicated with only three drinks in their system. For people with average weight (e.g., 140 to 180 pounds, 63 to 81 kg) four drinks in their system will produce a BAC of approximately .08% to .10%. People over 180 pounds (81 kg) can have as many as five drinks before becoming legally intoxicated according to the law.

However, whether or not you are legally intoxicated is not the real issue. *As you will see, impairment of skills begins well below the legal limit.*

sumed, it reaches the brain and begins to affect the drinker. Alcohol's major effect is to slow down and impair bodily functions—both mental and physical. Whatever you do, you do less well after consuming alcohol.

Blood Alcohol Concentration

The more alcohol in your blood, the greater the degree of impairment. Your body is able to eliminate alcohol at the rate of almost one drink per hour. If you consume at a rate *greater* than one drink an hour, alcohol will begin to accumulate in your body. The amount of alcohol in the body is referred to as Blood-Alcohol Concentration or BAC. At a BAC of between .08% and .10%, most people can no longer function normally and are, according to most state laws, intoxicated. But they are impaired long before reaching .08%. It begins with the first drink.

What Determines BAC

Three factors determine BAC:

- the amount of alcohol consumed.
- the number of hours drinking.
- body weight.

Alcohol and the Law

It is against the law to operate a motor vehicle while intoxicated—.08 or .10 percent, depending on your state. It doesn't matter how sober you may look or act, the breath test is what usually determines whether you are riding legally or illegally.

Your chances of being stopped for riding under the influence of alcohol are increasing. Law enforcement across the country has stepped up its efforts in response to the senseless deaths and injuries caused by drinking drivers.

Consequences of Conviction

Many years ago, first offenders had a good chance of getting off with a small fine and participation in drinking-drivers' classes. Today, the laws of most states impose stiff penalties on drinking drivers. And those penalties are mandatory, meaning that judges *must* impose them.

If you were convicted of riding while intoxicated, you could receive any of the following penalties.

- **Licensing suspension**—One- to six-month suspension for conviction, arrest, or refusal to submit to a breath test.
- **Incarceration**—Overnight jail stay.
- **Fines**—First-offense penalties ranging from $300 to $500; additional penalties ranging from $1,000 to $2,000.
- **Insurance**—A $500 to $1,000 increase in annual premiums.
- **Community service**—Fifty hours of community service performing tasks such as picking up litter along the highway, washing cars in the motor-vehicle pool, or working at an emergency ward.
- **Costs**—Additional costs such as lawyers' fees to pay; lost work time spent in court or alcohol-education programs; public transportation costs (while your license is suspended); and the added psychological cost of being tagged a "drunk driver."

Many over-the-counter and prescription drugs' side effects increase the risks of riding. The combined effects of alcohol and any drug are more dangerous than the effect of either one alone.

The Laws In Your State

You should know the laws that apply to alcohol and the operation of a motor vehicle in your state. If you do not know, phone the local Department of Motor Vehicles to determine:

- BAC intoxication levels: _____ percent
- Consequences of conviction for first offenders
- Consequences of subsequent convictions
- Consequences of refusing to take the blood alcohol test

Alcohol and Other Drugs In Motorcycle Operation

No one is immune to the effects of alcohol. No matter how much friends may brag about their ability to hold their liquor, alcohol makes them less able to think clearly and to perform physical tasks skillfully. Alcohol has extremely harmful effects on the processes involved in motorcycle operation, and these effects begin long before you are legally intoxicated.

Alcohol is not the only drug that affects your ability to ride safely. Many over-the-counter and prescription (as well as illegal) drugs have side effects that increase the risks of riding. While it is difficult to accurately measure the involvement of any particular drug in motorcycle accidents, it is known what effects various drugs have on the processes involved in riding a motorcycle. It's also known that the combined effects of alcohol and any drug are more dangerous than the effect of either one alone.

Alcohol/Drugs and Their Effect on Riding
What effect does alcohol have on mental and physical abilities? With *one to two drinks* in a person's system, mental processes such as restraint, awareness, concentration, and judgment are affected. Reaction time is slowed, and the person becomes unable to perform complicated tasks.

With *three to four drinks* in his or her system, a person's depth perception, glare recovery, eye movement, and focus are affected. There is a further decrease in judgment and control.

With *five drinks,* coordination deteriorates, critical judgment is lost, and memory and comprehension are impaired.

But what effects do other drugs have on the riding process?

Depressants, such as sedatives, barbiturates, and tranquilizers (quaalude, librium, red devils, PCP, or angel dust) cause confusion, lack of coordination, depression, drunken appearance, slurred speech, and a quick temper. These drugs impair every vital riding skill.

Stimulants, such as cocaine, speed, bennies, dexies, crystal, amphetamines, and benzedrine, may seem to make a person self-confident and alert. But this is often followed by depression and extreme fatigue when the drug wears off. Stimulants impair judgment of the riding environment, road-surface awareness, perception of other vehicles, turning-speed selection, and defensive-riding ability.

Marijuana (also known as grass, weed, or pot) alters a person's time/space perception and fragments thought. Reaction time increases, and immediate memory is impaired. This leads to impairment in road-surface awareness, scanning, perception of other vehicles, night vision, turning-speed selection, braking, defensive-riding abilities, and evasive maneuvering.

Heroin (commonly called H, horse, smack, or scag) causes tingling, drowsiness, daydreaming, stupor, and physical addiction. Heroin impairs every vital riding skill.

Minimizing the Risks
One of the functions that alcohol affects first is your ability to judge how well you are doing. This means that although you may be performing more and more poorly, you *think* you are doing better and better and you ride confidently into greater and greater risks. The best way to minimize the risks of drinking and riding is to take steps *before* you drink—either to control your drinking or to control your riding.

Controlling Drinking
- **Don't drink**—Once you start, your resistance becomes weaker and impairment begins.
- **Set a limit**—Decide beforehand to drink sparingly. Set a limit for yourself and stick to it. Best of all, don't drink if you're riding.
- **Find alternate activities**—Find other things to do besides drinking so you consume less.

Controlling Riding
If you haven't controlled your drinking, you must control your riding.
- **Leave the bike home**—When you know you will be drinking, leave the bike at home so you won't be tempted to ride. Arrange another way to get home.
- **Wait**—Once you have exceeded your limit, you will have to wait until your system eliminates the alcohol—wait at least one hour per drink. No other method will work!

Stepping In to Protect Friends
When people have had too much to drink to make a responsible decision themselves, it is up to others to step in and keep them from taking too great a risk. No one *wants* to do this—it's uncomfortable, embarrassing, and thankless. Your efforts are rarely appreciated at the time. But the alternatives are often worse.

There are several ways you can step in to keep friends from hurting themselves or wrecking their bikes.

- **Arrange a safe ride**—Provide alternative ways for them to get home.
- **Control their drinking**—Direct them by involving them in other activities.
- **Keep them there**—Use any excuse to keep them from getting on their bike if they've had too much. Serve them food and coffee to pass the time. Explain your concerns for their risks of getting arrested or wrecking their motorcycle.
- **Keep the bike there**—If you can't control the rider, control the bike. Take the keys or temporarily disable the bike (e.g., loosen or switch the plug leads enough so they won't fire).

It helps to enlist support from others when you decide to step in. The more people on your side, the easier it is to be firm and the harder it is for the drunk rider to resist. While you may not be thanked at the time, you will never have to say, "If only I had . . .

If friends are too intoxicated to make a responsible decision themselves, it is up to you to step in and keep them from taking too great a risk.

Self-Test for Chapter 4: Riding Straight

Answer "true" or "false" to each statement.

1. Alcohol and other drugs affect experienced riders' ability to ride safely less than novice riders. True or false?

2. There is alcohol involved in nearly half of all motorcyclist fatalities. True or false?

3. Your riding skills won't be impaired until your BAC reaches the legal limit. True or false?

4. Taking over-the-counter or prescription drugs can affect your riding abilities just as much as alcohol or illegal drugs. True or false?

(Answers appear on page 176.)

Protective Riding Gear

5

One of the things that makes motorcycling so enjoyable is the freedom of riding in the open air. Unlike car drivers surrounded by a steel compartment, motorcycle riders feel a part of everything around them. Of course, sometimes this can have its challenges: like riding in extremely cold or hot weather; when it's raining; when insects are about; or when debris flies up from the road. It's for these situations that proper riding gear is essential.

Riding gear has two basic purposes: comfort and protection. Uncomfortable gear can distract you from riding. High-quality riding gear will help you stay comfortable in all kinds of riding conditions and enhance the ride. In the event of an accident, proper riding gear helps prevent or reduce injuries.

Many activities or sports have their own suitable protective clothing and equipment. Motorcycling is no exception. Every rider and passenger should wear over-the-ankle footgear, long pants, a riding jacket, full-fingered leather gloves, and—above all—a helmet that meets U.S. Department of Transportation standards.

About Helmets

Helmets work. Helmet effectiveness has been confirmed by responsible studies, while helmet myths—such as helmets break necks, block vision, impair hearing, cause overheating, etc.—have been disproven time and time again. Informed riders wear helmets by deliberate choice every time they ride.

Look at what a helmet really does. First, it is the best protective gear you can wear while riding a motorcycle. Think of it at the same time you think of your ignition key. You pick up the key, you pick up the helmet. They go together.

Second, a good helmet makes riding a motorcycle more comfortable and therefore more fun. It cuts down on wind noise roaring by your ears, windblast on your face and eyes, and deflects bugs and other objects that fly through the air. It helps you cope with changing weather conditions and reduces rider fatigue.

Wearing a helmet, whether or not required by law, is a reflection of your attitude toward riding. And that attitude is plainly seen by other riders and non-riders alike.

How and Why a Helmet Works

Different helmets do different things. Motorcyclists, bicyclists, construction workers, and football players all have different needs. None are interchangeable. Motorcycle helmets are very sophisticated and specialized for the activity. They've been developed carefully and scientifically over the years.

Four basic components work together to provide protection: an outer shell, an impact-absorbing liner, comfort padding, and a good retention system.

What we see first is the **outer shell,** usually made of some group of fiber-reinforced composites: fiberglass or injection-molded plastic. This is tough stuff, but designed and intended to

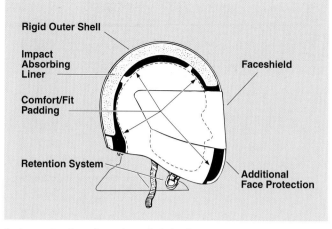

Basic construction of a motorcycle helmet

crunch when it hits anything hard. That action disperses energy from the impact to lessen the force before it reaches your head. But it can't act alone to protect you.

Inside the shell is the equally important **impact-absorbing liner,** usually made of expanded polystyrene. This dense layer cushions and absorbs the shock as the helmet stops but your head wants to continue moving.

Both the shell and the liner spread the forces of impact throughout the helmet's materials. The more impact energy that is deflected or absorbed, the less there is of it to reach your head and do damage. Helmet shells self-destruct to absorb impact energy by delaminating, cracking or breaking. This destruction means the shell is doing its intended job. Impact damage to the non-resilient liner may be invisible to the naked eye. The liner may look great, but may have little further protective value and should be replaced after a significant impact.

The **comfort padding** is the soft foam and cloth layer that sits next to your head. It helps keep you comfortable and the helmet fitting snugly. In some helmets, you can even take out this padding for cleaning.

The **retention system,** or chin strap, is very important. It is the one piece that keeps the helmet on your head in the event of a crash. A strap is connected to each side of the shell. Every time you put the helmet on, *fasten the straps securely.* It only takes a couple of seconds. To ride without the helmet securely strapped on would be as questionable as driving without a seatbelt fastened.

Choosing a Helmet

While color, design, and price may be a part of your decision on which helmet to buy, protection comes first. A full-coverage helmet gives the most protection since it covers more of your face. A movable faceshield protects your eyes and is easily operated with one hand. Professional and seasoned riders tend to prefer full-face helmets for the added protection and comfort.

A three-quarter, open-face helmet is also a choice of some riders. It is constructed with the same basic components, but doesn't offer the face and chin protection of full-face helmets. Snap-on faceshields provide eye protection, but won't withstand the impact of a crash. At the very least you should wear a pair of goggles that can withstand impacts. Ordinary glasses or sunglasses are not sufficient eye protection for a motorcyclist; they might shatter, move, or fly off.

Goggles provide eye protection, but they don't protect from possible injury to other areas of the face. Full-coverage helmets provide better protection.

Before purchasing goggles, be sure "VESC-8" is inscribed on them. This signifies that they meet the Vehicle Equipment Safety Commission's standards for optical properties and strength. Goggles should be securely fastened over the helmet so they do not blow off. A face guard should allow airflow to the face for comfort, easy breathing, and to prevent fogging. Most frames have a rubber/cotton-fiber strap that resists tearing and stretching. Goggles can be washed by hand in the sink then hung up to dry.

A wide variety of good helmets are available today, in all price ranges. One look around a dealer's helmet display reveals that nearly any

Research Confirms Helmet Effectiveness . . .

There's no better expert on the protective value and effectiveness of helmets than David Thom.

What makes him an expert? A miraculous experience in which a helmet saved his life? A likely guess, but if that were the case then there would be countless helmet "experts."

While Thom has done his share of personal crash testing over the years, his occupation makes him an unquestionable authority on motorcycle helmets, and protective headgear in general. Who can doubt the director of the University of Southern California's Head Protection Research Laboratory?

Thom has been at the facility since 1977, when he came on board as a motorcycle specialist to assist in collecting data for the landmark study by Professor Harry Hurt, *Motorcycle Accident Cause Factors and Identification of Countermeasures* (also known as "The Hurt Study"). Since that time, Thom estimates he's examined 2,500 motorcycle accidents, with 1,200 to 1,400 of those involving helmeted riders. After a crash, Thom and his student interns evaluate the helmet's performance relative to the injuries, if any, that the motorcyclist received.

"Most of the time when people wear a helmet, fall off a motorcycle, and bonk their head on the ground, they don't have any injuries," Thom says. "That's the routine accident. They hurt their helmet but not their head."

As the numerous helmets hanging on the lab's office walls attest, there have been many accidents to study. While the USC team still observes routine accidents, the emphasis has shifted to the instances where helmeted riders receive a head injury in a crash. Such crashes typically involve much higher energy and can be violent accidents. In such cases, the helmet damage is evaluated relative to the head injury sustained.

According to Thom, wearing a helmet that meets U.S. Department of Transportation (DOT) standards will adequately protect riders in the majority of crashes. DOT has rigid standards for impact, penetration, retention, and vision properties that motorcycle helmets sold in the U.S. must meet.

"When you fall and hit your head, you will hit with an impact energy that is less than the DOT standard 90% of the time," says Thom, who often tests helmets on lab equipment that replicates the DOT testing apparatus.

Helmet manufacturers that comply with the standards place DOT stickers on the backs of their helmets as well as more detailed information on the inside. Recently "novelty" helmet manufacturers have begun placing DOT stickers on helmets that *don't* comply with the standards. These lids may resemble a regular helmet with their hard, shiny shells. But underneath there is no impact-absorbing polystyrene, and the chin straps are often thin and attached poorly to the shell.

"People need to be aware that if they get a helmet that weighs one pound, just covers the very top of their head and has no thickness, it's not a real helmet," warns Thom. "No matter what anybody might tell you, you don't want to wear one of those. You will get no protection from it if you fall."

(continued)

color, decoration, and design on a helmet is available. Many manufacturers color-coordinate their helmets with the newest motorcycle models.

Modern helmets are made of new lightweight materials. The manufacturers constantly work to make them more protective and more comfortable.

The way to find a well-made, reliable helmet is to look for the DOT or SNELL sticker inside or outside the helmet. The sticker means the helmet complies with the safety-test standards of the U.S. Department of Transportation (DOT) and/or the Snell Memorial Foundation.

Each organization has rigid standards for:

Impact—the shock-absorbing capacity of the helmet.

Penetration—the helmet's ability to withstand a blow from a sharp object.

Retention—the chin strap's ability to stay fastened without breaking or stretching.

Peripheral Vision—the helmet must provide a minimum side vision of 105 degrees to each side. (Most people's usable peripheral vision is only about 90 degrees to each side.)

Since 1980, *all* helmets for on-highway use must meet DOT standards. Helmet dealers and distributors must ensure that all the helmets they sell bear the DOT sticker. When choosing a helmet, be sure it has this certification. You don't want an inferior helmet or one designed for another purpose. If someone tries to sell you one without it, don't buy it. If you have one without it, the helmet is probably so old it should be replaced anyway.

Snell has been testing helmets since the 1950s. The use of Snell standards by helmet manufacturers is voluntary, unlike DOT standards. Snell testing is of high quality and is revised (most recently in 1990) as helmet design and technology improve. To ensure continued compliance, Snell periodically spot checks helmets they have approved.

Both agencies attempt to reproduce, under test conditions, the situations that are hazardous to motorcyclists. Their testing methods differ,

but the intent is the same: to make certain any helmet they approve has life-saving, shock-absorbing minimum qualities.

Since head injuries account for a majority of motorcycle fatalities, head protection is vital. Even the best helmet is no guarantee against injury. However, without a helmet you are five times more likely to have serious head injuries than a helmeted rider.

Getting the Right Fit

There's more to fitting a helmet than just buying the one that matches your hat size or guessing at "small, medium, or large." Your hat size is a good starting point, however. Measure your head at its largest circumference—usually just above the eyebrows in front, over your ears and around in back. Try it several times so you know you've gotten the largest number. Then convert from inches or centimeters to hat size, using the chart below:

Inches	cm	Hat Size
21 $\frac{1}{4}$	54	6 $\frac{3}{4}$
21 $\frac{5}{8}$	54.9	6 $\frac{7}{8}$
22	55.9	7
22 $\frac{3}{8}$	56.8	7 $\frac{1}{8}$
22 $\frac{3}{4}$	57.8	7 $\frac{1}{4}$
23 $\frac{1}{8}$	58.7	7 $\frac{3}{8}$
23 $\frac{1}{2}$	59.7	7 $\frac{1}{2}$
23 $\frac{7}{8}$	60.6	7 $\frac{5}{8}$
24 $\frac{1}{4}$	61.6	7 $\frac{3}{4}$
24 $\frac{3}{4}$	62.8	7 $\frac{7}{8}$

Since some helmets are simply marked as S, M, L, or XL, you may need to contact the manufacturer for size equivalents. Unfortunately, they vary.

A helmet should fit snugly and may even feel a bit too tight until it's in place correctly. It should sit squarely on your head, not tilted back like a hat. The cheek pads should touch your cheeks without pressing uncomfortably.

There should be no gaps between your temples and the brow pads.

. . . Research Confirms Helmet Effectiveness . . .

Some partial-coverage helmets are DOT approved. They will have about one inch (2.5 cm) of polystyrene underneath the shell, a sturdy fastening system, and cover more than just the very top of your head.

"Although a partial-coverage helmet provides a high level of protection compared to nothing, it is definitely not as good as a helmet that has more coverage, particularly a full-face helmet with polystyrene in the chin bar," Thom said.

Many people turn to Thom for a recommendation on the best helmet on the market.

"There really isn't an answer," he says.

Some cost more than others. But according to Thom, you can get virtually the same protection from a DOT-approved $100 helmet as you can from a brand-name model costing up to $500. It's all in the helmet's construction.

Some helmet-making processes cost more. Take the shell, for example. A fiberglass shell costs more to make than an injection-molded polycarbonate shell. As long as the shell helps to spread the initial impact to a wider area of the underlying liner, it doesn't matter which material is used.

Comfort features, such as special vent systems and interior padding, add to the price. So do special factory paint schemes and scratch-resistant, quick-change faceshields.

The comfort and appearance features are what separate adequate helmets from exceptional helmets.

David Thom, director of the University of Southern California's Head Protection Research Laboratory, often tests helmets on lab equipment that replicates the DOT testing apparatus.

"Some helmets are a little better at some things than others," says Thom. "Except for fake helmets." he quickly adds, "They're not good for anything."

(continued)

With the helmet still on and straps securely fastened, move it from side to side and up and down. If it fits right, your skin should move as the helmet is moved. You should feel as if a slight, even pressure is being exerted all over your head by the helmet.

A helmet will loosen up slightly as the comfort liner compresses through use. So a new one should be as tight as you can comfortably wear.

With the chin strap securely fastened and your head straight, the helmet shouldn't roll forward off your head. If you can pull it off, the helmet is too big.

A helmet that is too large will move around and up and down on your head. This could be hazardous if the helmet were to move and block your vision. Plus it can be very annoying to wear because it's noisy and lets in wind. And, in the event of an accident, it is likely to come off!

After removing the helmet, note any soreness or red spots on your forehead. Pressure points can be uncomfortable and can cause a headache after a long ride, so be sure the helmet doesn't cause any. If it does, choose the next larger size or try a different brand of helmet. Human heads are not all the same shape; neither are helmets.

Each time you ride, you're going to be spending time with that helmet. Do you want one that fits poorly? Of course not! When you put on your helmet, you want the same comfy feeling that you get from the La-Z-Boy recliner in your living room. Allow plenty of time in the shop when purchasing your helmet. Wear the helmet around a while. A helmet is an important investment, no matter what its price.

Tips on Helmet Care

Follow the manufacturer's directions on caring for your helmet. Use only the mildest soap recommended for cleaning. Avoid any petroleum-based cleaning fluids, especially on a polycarbonate helmet. Exposure to strong cleaning agents can cause the helmet to decompose and lose protective value.

Keep your helmet's faceshield clean. Normally, mild soap and water with a soft cloth will do the job. If it gets scratched, use plastic polish or replace it. A scratched faceshield reduces vision, especially at night when the scratches distort oncoming lights.

Helmets look tough and sturdy, but should be handled as fragile items. Dropping a helmet onto a hard surface could ruin it. Remember that its function is to absorb impact in an accident.

It is not wise to store helmets near gasoline, cleaning fluids, exhaust fumes or excessive heat. Helmet materials can react chemically to these factors. Damage done this way may be noticeable, but most often is invisible. Read the information that comes with the helmet so you know how to care for it.

Definitely read the instructions about painting, decorating, pinstriping, or applying decals to your helmet. Some thermoplastic or polycarbonate helmet compositions can be changed if painted or if decals are applied.

Never hang a helmet on the motorcycle's mirrors, turn signals, or sissy bar. The inner liner can easily be damaged from such handling. In fact, avoid carrying a spare helmet on your motorcycle, unless it's well protected or on your passenger's head. Even the bumps and jarring from normal riding can damage a spare helmet. If it is strapped on or near hot engine parts or exhaust pipes, the inner liner may distort or melt at the hot spot.

Another reason not to hang your helmet from the mirrors or handgrips is to prevent damage to the outer shell. Anything new and shiny seems to be a target for Murphy's Law ("Anything that can go wrong, will go wrong"). Ever notice how a runaway grocery cart finds the newest car in the parking lot? Or your brand-new skis find the rocks on the slope? Or the spaghetti sauce jumps onto your clean shirt? Don't tempt fate!

If you plan to use a CB radio or interactive communications system when you ride, find a model that doesn't require drilling speaker holes in your helmet's structure. (Before you purchase

. . . Research Confirms Helmet Effectiveness

Features like the special vent systems and interior padding shown here add to the comfort and the price of a helmet. ∎

The USC team has studied thousands of helmets that were worn in accidents. "Most of the time when people wear a helmet, fall off a motorcycle, and bonk their head on the ground, they don't have any injuries," Thom says.

Riding boots should cover your ankles and have non-slip soles. Shown are boots designed for racing, left, and touring, right.

speakers, check your state's laws regulating their use in helmets. Some states prohibit them.)

Replacing a Helmet

Plan to replace a helmet if it is involved in an accident—it probably absorbed some impact shock. Some helmet manufacturers will inspect and, when possible, repair a damaged helmet. If you drop your helmet and think it might be damaged, take advantage of this service.

Most helmet manufacturers recommend replacing your helmet every two to four years. If you notice any signs of damage before then, replace it sooner.

Why replace a helmet every few years if it doesn't appear damaged? Its protective qualities may deteriorate with wear and exposure to sunlight. The chin strap may fray or loosen at its attaching points. Probably the best reason, however, is that helmets keep improving. Chances are, helmets available in a couple of years will be better, stronger, lighter, and more comfortable than those on the market now. They might even cost less!

If you can't remember when you bought your present helmet, check the chin strap or permanent labeling. Since 1974, all helmets must have the month and date of production stamped on them.

State Helmet Requirements

Many states require a specific amount of retroreflective material on a helmet. Check with the dealer to be sure the helmet you plan to purchase meets the requirements. Again, read the manufacturer's information. Your local motor-vehicle department can give you exact information on the location and amount of retroreflective material required in your state.

You've now read that there are many things to consider when buying a helmet. Get *all* the information you can. Talk with an MSF-certified *RiderCourse* Instructor, your local motorcycle dealer, and other riders. Contact helmet manufacturers and read their literature. Consult recent motorcycle-enthusiast magazines for up-to-date information to help in your decision. Two agencies you can contact are:

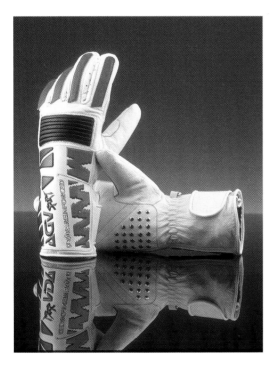

For the greatest comfort, buy gloves made especially for motorcyclists. At left are racing gloves; at right, insulated gloves for winter.

- National Highway Traffic Safety
    Administration
  Traffic Safety Programs
  Office of Occupant Protection
  400 7th Street Southwest
  Washington, DC 20590
  (202) 366-1739
- Snell Memorial Foundation, Inc.
  Box 493
  St. James, NY 11780

Other Riding Gear

Footwear

Over-the-ankle leather boots protect you from a variety of riding hazards. They protect ankles from stones that are thrown up from the roadway and prevent burns from hot exhaust pipes. Rubber-soled boots will help provide a strong grip on the pavement at intersections and help keep your feet on the pegs while riding.

In case of an accident or spill, boots provide valuable protection against foot and ankle injuries.

Gloves

Leather gloves protect hands from blisters and the wind, sun, and cold. In the event of a crash, gloves help prevent cuts and bruises to your hands. Gloves that fit snugly will improve your grip on the handlebars.

If gloves are too bulky, they may create problems in operating the motorcycle controls. If they are too tight, circulation will be restricted and your hands will become cold. Seamless gloves will help prevent blisters. Gauntlets will keep cold air from going up jacket sleeves. Lighter gloves are good for summer; heavier, well-insulated gloves should be worn in winter.

Clothing

Good clothing will help you stay comfortable while riding in all conditions. In case of an accident, high-quality riding clothes will prevent or reduce injury.

Clothing sold specifically for motorcycling gives you the best combination of fit and protection. These garments are designed to fit while you're sitting in a riding position. They are cut longer in the sleeves and legs and are fuller across the shoulders and longer in the back. Flaps and fasteners seal out the wind while extra padding provides crash protection.

(Left) Extra padding at the shoulders, elbows, and knees provides protection in case of a crash.

(Right) Leather is durable, wind resistant, and protects against injury. Riding pants are narrow so they don't become entangled in parts of the motorcycle.

Leather clothing is favored by many riders because it is durable, wind resistant, and gives good protection against injury and the cold. There are alternative high-tech fabrics on the market that provide protection similar to leather. Other fabrics offer adequate protection and are less expensive than leather. If you are considering buying a jacket or suit made of one of these materials, make sure it is strong enough to resist abrasion. Even denim can provide adequate protection in a fall.

Avoid wide-flared pants, flowing scarves, and similar items because they could become entangled in the chain, spokes, or other parts of the motorcycle.

A jacket with a zippered front will be more wind resistant than a jacket with buttons or snaps. A flap of material over the jacket's zipper gives additional protection against the wind. Jackets with snug cuffs and waist are recommended to keep wind from blowing into the garment. Be careful about collar style—a large, loose collar will flap when riding and may irritate skin or be a distraction. Motorcycle clothing should fit comfortably without binding.

Remember that even in warm weather, constant exposure to wind when riding may cause hypothermia, a subnormal body temperature. Hypothermia can cause you to lose your ability to concentrate and react to changing traffic conditions. Motorcyclists are especially susceptible to rapid chilling leading to loss of reflexes, a symptom of hypothermia. The biggest danger of hypothermia is deterioration of the ability to think clearly. Proper riding gear, such as a windproof jacket and insulated layers of clothing, is essential.

On a slightly cool day (65 degrees Fahrenheit, 18 degrees Celsius), a motorcyclist riding at highway speeds of 45 to 55 miles per hour (72 to 88 KPH) experiences a temperature equivalent of 33 degrees Fahrenheit (one degree Celsius). That's only one degree above freezing. Riders

Bogus Helmets

How can you tell if that helmet is bogus? Here's a brief history, and a short list of requirements.

The National Highway Traffic Safety Administration issued Federal Motor Vehicle Safety Standard Number 218, Motorcycle Helmets, in 1973. It was most recently amended in 1988.

FMVSS No. 218 establishes performance requirements. There is also a section that explains the labeling requirements. The label must be permanent and legible, so that it can be read easily without removing the padding or other permanent part. It must include the manufacturer's name or identification, the precise model designation, the size, the month and year of manufacture (for example, June 1992 or 6/92), and the symbol DOT. By printing DOT on the label, the manufacturer is certifying that the helmet conforms to FMVSS No. 218. The DOT symbol must appear on the outer surface, in a color that contrasts with the background, in letters at least $\frac{3}{8}$-inch high.

The label must also include:

- Shell constructed of polystyrene foam and liner constructed of [material].
- Helmet can be seriously damaged by some common substances without damage being visible to the user. Apply only the following: [Cleaning agents, paints, adhesives, etc., recommended by manufacturers].
- Make no modifications. Fasten helmet securely. If helmet experiences a severe blow, return it to the manufacturer for inspection, or destroy it and replace it.

Any additional relevant information will be on a tag or a brochure.

If there is a DOT label on the lower back of the helmet, but you suspect it does not meet FMVSS No. 218, inspect the inside of the helmet. Has the manufacturer complied with the other labeling requirements, described above? If not, it does not meet FMVSS No. 218 standards.

Also, helmets may have labels from the American National Standards Institute (ANSI) or the Snell Memorial Foundation. ANSI and Snell have somewhat different requirements. The DOT standard is the only one the helmet is required to meet by law.

■

skin quickens dehydration, and a jacket helps protect your skin from drying wind. Stay away from jackets made of extremely thin material. They will flap too easily in the wind.

On hot, sunny days, it is best to wear light colored clothes and helmet. Lighter colors reflect the sun's rays, rather than absorbing them like darker colors. This can make a difference of 10 degrees F (12 degrees C) or more on hot days.

The clothes you wear while riding can make you more visible in traffic. Choose brightly colored clothing when possible. If you wear dark clothing, you can wear an inexpensive retroreflective vest over the jacket. Also, it is a good idea to affix reflectorized tape striping to garments you wear regularly when riding. This applies to bright clothing worn during the day. Unless they are reflectorized, they will not offer the same good visibility at night. Jackets made of retroreflective material also will help make you more visible once the sun sets.

Rainsuits

For the avid motorcycle rider, a rainsuit is a must. A dry motorcyclist will be much more comfortable and alert than one who is wet and cold.

One- or two-piece rainsuits can be purchased in several materials, the most common being polyvinyl chloride and nylon. They come in different colors, but orange or yellow is best for high visibility.

There are usually only small differences in rainsuit styles. The pants to a typical rainsuit have elastic at the waist and stirrups (or tie-strings) on the pant legs to wrap around your boots. The jacket should have a high collar. The front zips up and a wide flap fastens across the opening. The wrist openings are held tightly with more elastic or adjustable tabs.

When purchasing a rainsuit, also consider purchasing glove and boot covers. Most glove covers are large enough to fit over gauntlet-type gloves without interfering with hand flexibility. The boot covers have tie-strings on top and should be worn under the pants. The pant stir-

not dressed properly for the chill could suffer the effects of hypothermia.

Clothes that are just right for cold-weather riding may be too hot once you stop riding. To prevent this, dress in layers so that you can remove outer clothing as needed.

When preparing to ride in cold weather, several layers of clothing are necessary, usually starting with thermal underwear. Extra layers of pants, shirts, and jackets should be layered loosely to aid body heat in forming warm insulation. Topping your clothing with a windproof outer layer will prevent the cold wind from reaching your body.

Insulated riding suits offer another alternative in cold weather. These lightweight suits provide the warmth needed to prevent hypothermia. Another option available to motorcyclists is an electrically warmed vest or suit.

Regardless of temperature, you should always wear at least a lightweight jacket. This reduces the chance of becoming dehydrated while riding on a hot day. Wind rushing over exposed rups are pulled over the boot covers. The boot covers will not tolerate much abuse, so we suggest you take them off before walking.

You've prepared your mind for the ride ahead. You're outfitted in the proper riding attire—"armored and ready." But there's still one more thing to do before starting your journey—prepare your motorcycle.

Rainsuits are available in both one-piece (center) and two-piece styles. The jacket should have a high collar and a wide flap that fastens snugly across the front.

Self-Test for Chapter 5: Protective Riding Gear

Choose the best answer for each question.

1. What are the two functions of riding gear?

   _____

   _____

2. How does a good helmet make riding more comfortable and therefore more fun?

   a. Reduces wind noise/windblast.
   b. Helps prevent heat loss through your head.
   c. Deflects insects and other flying debris.
   d. All of the above.

3. If you crash while not wearing a helmet, how many times more likely are you to suffer serious head injuries than if you were wearing a helmet?

   a. 2.
   b. 5.
   c. 10.
   d. The risk is the same.

4. Why should you wear at least a lightweight jacket while riding on a hot day?

   a. It can actually help keep you cooler.
   b. Wearing a jacket protects your skin from drying wind, reducing the risk of dehydration.
   c. A jacket blocks the sun.
   d. All of the above.

   (Answers appear on page 176.)

Motorcycle Inspection, Care, and Troubleshooting

6

When you consider how much enjoyment your motorcycle brings you, you probably don't mind that it needs more frequent attention than your car. A minor technical failure in a car seldom leads to anything more than an inconvenience for the driver. Such a failure can be deadly to the motorcyclist.

Many longtime riders have at least one tale of an old, temperamental motorcycle. But the reliability of today's machines have made getting stranded on the roadside a rare occurrence.

You can ride more confidently knowing that you've paid close attention to every aspect of your motorcycle's mechanical well-being. Regular maintenance and preventive care can go a long way toward ensuring a trouble-free ride. But sometimes even the best-kept motorcycle can develop a problem. Many times you can see a potential problem developing, and it's in your best interest to solve it before minor trouble becomes a major crisis on the highway. Therefore, it's important to check your machine before every ride.

Motorcycles don't wear out overnight, of course, but a daily check of your machine's general condition and fluid levels can make your ride a safer one. A pre-ride check can be a quick and easy inspection of critical components, easily remembered using the term T-CLOCK.

T stands for tires and wheels. Probably the most common problem that can leave you stranded is a flat tire. There is no way to predict when you might run over a nail. But there are signs to look for to prevent a tire failure, or blowout. Before each ride, inspect the tire's tread for depth, wear, cuts, embedded objects, bulges, and weathering.

Maintaining proper air pressure is especially important, so be sure to check it before each ride. If necessary, adjust the pressure to the manufacturer's recommendations. If, under normal loads and operation, a tire needs air every time you ride, suspect a small puncture or impending failure and immediately replace it. Incorrect pressure can lead to uneven wear. Low pressure causes excessive heat buildup or instability, especially when carrying extra loads, which can lead to tire failure.

Most tires have small "wear bars" built into the tread grooves. When these bars appear, the tread is gone and you should replace the tire. Although it may look like a sufficient amount of tread remains, it won't be enough to maintain traction in wet conditions. (This is explained further in a later chapter on traction). Plus, worn tires are easier to puncture.

While you're inspecting the tires, put the motorcycle on its centerstand and check the wheels as well. Many modern motorcycles come with cast-spoke wheels. You'll want to be sure these wheels are free of cracks or dents. With a traditional spoked wheel you must be sure the spokes remain tight. Regardless of the type of wheel, be sure the rim is straight and round. Check the wheel bearings for wear by grasping the tire at the top and bottom then pushing and pulling.

Proper tire air pressure prevents uneven wear, heat buildup, and instability.

Check your bike's wheel bearings by grasping the tire at the top and bottom, then push and pull. There should be no free play or noise.

GOOD   BAD

Inspect the wheel-bearing seals for cracks and discoloration.

There should be no free play or audible noise from the hub or axle. Also inspect the seals for cracks and discoloration.

Fully loaded motorcycles are particularly hard on tires and wheels. The extra weight puts a greater load on wheel bearings, spokes, rims, tires, and tubes. Extra maintenance of these items is essential when carrying such loads.

C stands for controls—levers, cables, hoses, and throttle. Be sure the levers are tight in the mounts but pivot freely, and are free of cracks. Look for signs of fraying in the cables and check their routing so that there are no kinks. Control cables usually fray before breaking completely. If a cable begins to fray, its action will likely feel gritty and rough.

Check the throttle cable so that it doesn't pull when the handlebars turn. The throttle should rotate freely on the handlebars and snap closed when released. If you notice the throttle sticking open, try closing it manually. Many new motorcycles have a second cable to close the throttle. If this works, be sure to immediately service the cable so that it automatically snaps closed when the grip is released. If the throttle sticks while you're riding, you'll have to use the clutch and engine cut-off switch to safely maneuver out of traffic to where you can stop.

Cable ends sometimes come off unexpectedly. For long-distance touring, it might be a good idea to bring spare cables along just in case one breaks. They're cheap compared to the inconvenience of a breakdown.

If your motorcycle has hydraulic hoses, inspect them for cracks, cuts, leaks, bulges, chafing, and deterioration.

L is for lights and electrics. The electrical system is frequently neglected, which can lead to electrical failure. Electrical components are subject to vibration and bad weather, so it's vital to inspect them regularly.

Make sure your headlight, both high and low beams, works properly and is aimed correctly. Check your tail light and brake light.

Your bike won't run without electrical current, so keep the battery electrolyte level full and the battery terminals clean and tight. Many times loss of electrical power can be traced to loose or corroded battery connections.

Inspect electrical wiring for cracks, fraying, mounting, and chafing of the insulation. Look for disconnected or broken wires.

O is for oils and fluids. Keep the engine oil filled to the proper level and change it at regular intervals. This is perhaps the best maintenance you can perform for your engine. After a couple of thousand miles, the molecules in oil begin to break down and the oil loses its effectiveness to properly lubricate. In most motorcycle engines, the engine oil also lubricates the transmission. The extra stress of lashing gears puts further load on the oil molecules, making regular oil changes that much more critical.

Engines break in times of high stress such as over-revving, overloading, and when vital lubricants are either low or are too old and worn out. Engine failure often follows long-term symptoms such as poor starting, sluggish throttle response, and unusual noises.

Also look for gasket leaks at the engine cases. And don't forget to check brake and other hydraulic-fluid levels.

If your motorcycle is liquid cooled, inspect the coolant level at the reservoir or recovery tank. Also be sure to check the radiator and hoses for cracks or other signs of leakage.

Don't forget your fuel system. Be sure fuel filters don't become clogged with dirt. Replace them according to your owner's manual. If your bike has a fuel petcock, it should turn from OFF to ON to RESERVE smoothly. A leaky petcock will allow fuel to flow into the carburetors and possibly overfill or "flood" them. Some bikes may even leak if left in the ON position.

The other C stands for chassis and chain. Look for cracks at the frame's gussets and accessory mounts. Raise the front wheel off the ground and check the steering head for play and ease of movement. Raise the rear wheel and check for

Levers should be tight in the mounts, but pivot freely. Lubricate according to the owner's manual.

Make sure both the high and low beams of the headlight work properly. Check the tail light, too.

Keep the engine oil filled to the proper level and change it at regular intervals.

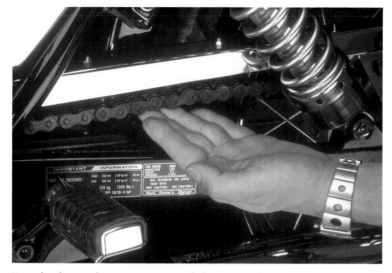

Keep the chain at the proper tension and alignment (refer to your owner's manual), and lubricate it often.

play in the swingarm by pushing/pulling on the wheel. Once both ends are back on the ground, check the suspension for smooth movement.

Motorcycle chains require frequent attention for long life and optimum service. It is essential to keep the chain at the proper tension and alignment, so be sure to refer to your owner's manual and perform the procedure when necessary. Depending on the riding conditions, you may need to lubricate it often as well. This is best done at the end of a ride when the chain is hot. Direct the chain lube into the side plates, not down the center of the rollers.

A badly worn chain is likely to break or derail and should be replaced. Not only will a broken chain leave you stranded by the side of the road, it can also fly off and injure you or your passenger. Broken chains can also do great damage to engine cases and swingarms.

Replace your chain when you can pull it away from the rear sprocket and expose more than half a tooth; if it is rusted, pitted, or cracked; has numerous kinked "tight spots;" or if the rear axle adjusters have reached their farthest limits. If you are unsure of your chain's condition, see your dealer.

Also inspect the sprockets for wear. Look for hooked or broken teeth, and keep the rear sprocket secured to the wheel hub. On a belt-driven engine, check for cracking, fraying, or missing teeth.

K is for the kickstand. Be sure the sidestand and centerstand spring up and out of the way when riding. Dangling stands can catch the pavement when leaning into a turn and cause a crash. (Most modern bikes' engines will not start if the stand is down and the transmission is in gear.)

And if you crash, it's especially important to thoroughly inspect your motorcycle before putting it on the road again. Pay close attention to moving parts, such as steering and suspension. You want to check for binding that could signal a bent fork leg or frame. Although minor misalignments in such parts as the handlebars or footpegs can be tolerated in an emergency ride home, any damage that interferes with the free movement of controls is an invitation to disaster and should be repaired before attempting to ride.

If your bike so much as merely falls over on the right side, you should immediately inspect the throttle. Underneath the grip is a plastic tube that pulls the throttle cable. This tube can splinter in a fall and jam the throttle on. It can also be easily pushed against the handlebar end and bind. Simply loosening the screws and relocating it in the proper position can often fix this problem. Don't let a stuck throttle, or any other crash damage, set you up for another fall.

The T-CLOCK inspection is most effective if performed when your bike is clean. Dirt, grease, and "road scum" can easily hide potential problems. Regular cleaning not only keeps your motorcycle looking new, but actually extends its life by cleansing and protecting it from the corrosive elements of the road.

No matter what you do, you can't prevent certain parts from wearing. But by replacing worn parts *before* they break, you may stop them from causing extensive damage by breaking several other parts along with them.

Be sure to follow the manufacturer's recommended maintenance schedule. This will keep your motorcycle running at peak performance and reduce the chances of mechanical failure. Keep a detailed maintenance record—it not only shows when the maintenance was performed, but it can add value to your motorcycle should you sell it.

Some routine maintenance procedures are simple. Others require the expertise of a trained technician. If you are unsure of your ability to perform any procedure, take your motorcycle to an authorized dealer. Remember, a mechanical problem incorrectly repaired can cause more extensive damage, which could ultimately lead to a crash.

How well you ride depends on how well your motorcycle performs. And that depends on the quality of care you provide.

Now that you and your motorcycle are ready to ride, let's consider the strategies that will help keep you safe on the street.

The owner's manual is an invaluable source of information, from the recommended maintenance schedule to setting your motorcycle's suspension, as shown.

Self-Test for Chapter 6:
Motorcycle Inspection, Care, and Troubleshooting

1. The term T-CLOCK can help you remember each part of your pre-ride check. What does each letter stand for?

   T_____ & _____
   C_____
   L_____ & _____
   O_____ & _____
   C_____ & _____
   K_____

Answer "true" or "false" to the following statements.

2. Low tire pressures always offer increased traction. True or false?

3. Motorcycle chains will last longer with frequent lubrication and careful adjustment. True or false?

4. Regular cleaning can help extend the life of your motorcycle. True or false?

(Answers appear on page 176.)

PART II

Get Set: Street Strategies for Smart Riders

Street Strategies and the Visual Edge

7

On the streets, situations change abruptly and constantly. As a skilled rider, you need to be in full control of your motorcycle. You must also be aware of your riding environment—what is happening around you and what is about to happen. Your riding skills must be second nature because your mind will be busy thinking about how to make yourself more visible to motorists, how to position yourself in traffic, and how to predict and deal with potential hazards.

Your street strategies are mental guidelines for the decisions you face on the streets.

Visibility

See and be seen—or, as some people call it, visibility. Research continues to tell us that it's the most important part of any riding strategy. Many motorcycle accidents are a result of motorists not seeing a motorcyclist until it is too late. Because motorcycles are smaller than automobiles, they can be more difficult to see and their speed may be more difficult to judge. In fact, automobile drivers often are not looking for motorcycles.

Being Seen

It is your responsibility to make yourself "seen" and to communicate your presence and intentions to other road users. There are several things you can do to accomplish this.

Wear bright clothing and a light-colored helmet. Use retroreflective material on your clothing, helmet, and motorcycle to increase your visibility in low-light conditions.

Ride with your headlight on high beam during the daytime. You might consider a modulator that pulses the headlight during daylight hours, if it's legal in your state.

Communicate with other drivers by signaling your intentions. Combine hand with electric signals whenever possible. And remember to cancel your turn signals. A false signal is as hazardous as none at all.

Learn how other drivers react to your motorcycle and your signals. To help avoid conflicts, practice rider-to-driver communication. When you need to make a lane change, use your turn signal then check to see if the driver behind you has reacted. Don't rely on the other driver "seeing" you.

A flashing light is more visible than a steady one. Flash the brake light before and during stops to make yourself more conspicuous to following traffic and to communicate your intentions.

Use the horn to gain attention, but don't rely on it. Most horns cannot be heard over traffic noise and a four-speaker stereo.

Seeing

The active part of visibility is your looking for and seeing the things that can affect you—gathering information through your eyes. In essence, this is "searching" everywhere and "seeing" only what is important. This process is scanning: an aggressive search for potential hazards.

Mental Systems

We live in the computer age. These machines have become a part of our lives. You may even own a computer. Even if you don't, things like Macintosh, IBM compatible, RAM, and hard drive are household words. Remember when "nets" were used to catch fish, and traps were used to catch "mice"?

We generally associate computers with what they do more than what they are. Few people deal on a daily basis with the complex programming that ultimately becomes the word processors, spreadsheets, databases, or games that you use. The logic—and even the language—would baffle most of us.

But some would say that there are only three things you must know to understand computers. First, computers are dumb. Without input, they can do nothing. Second, they are literal. They must be told exactly what to do and how to do it. Third, they are fast. They perform calculations at impressive rates.

Riding a motorcycle is mostly mental. Your brain manages the time and space that make up your riding environment. Mental systems are used for this purpose, just as a computer uses software programs for tasks such as word processing. But there are some big differences between your brain and a computer. Unlike the computer, you can decide what needs to be done. You are also capable of making decisions or even deciding if decisions need to be made. A relatively simple computer could operate the controls enough to make a bike start, turn, shift, and stop. But even the most elementary tasks in riding a motorcycle on the street require levels of processing that the most advanced computer could not handle.

On the street, no two situations are ever the same. Your ability to process information and manage time and space are based on countless sources of input that include experience, knowledge, skill training, and accurate interpretation from your senses. It sounds like a complicated situation, and it is! It's possible for much of the routine processing to take place subconsciously. It can become nearly automatic. Your brain, however, is capable of bringing critical information and the need for management into your consciousness.

Think for a moment how computers receive information. Very often, it's through a single source—most likely the keyboard. The computer uses this information with data already on hand to accomplish a task. But when you ride a motorcycle, your main source of information comes from your vision. Not only from what you see, but from your ability to place meaning on what you see. That's the mental system.

And your system is unique. ∎

You should be especially aware at intersections, where other vehicles can cross your path of travel. There are many things to scan for, including road surfaces; the traffic around you; and pedestrians.

Scanning covers more than just what is in front of you. You must be aware of what is to either side and behind you. Don't let your eyes fix on any one object for more than a split second. This will help you be aware of anything that may affect you. Scan a 12-to-14-second path of travel. This means looking ahead to an area it would take you 12 seconds to reach. This will give you time to prepare for a situation before it is in your immediate path of travel, the area four seconds ahead of you. Situations within this area require your immediate response.

Gather information about roadside and road surfaces: trees can shelter damp or icy spots in their shade; potholes can spread loose gravel on the road. Look at the movement of the traffic around you: cars ahead, behind, and beside you. Remember that intersections, where other vehicles can cross your path of travel, are especially critical. And don't overlook pedestrians and animals.

Include your rearview mirrors in your scanning, but don't rely on them. Turn your head to check the blind spots your mirrors will miss, especially when changing lanes, turning, or stopping.

Be extra alert at intersections where other vehicles can cross your path. Driveways, parking lots, and side streets can quickly develop into problems.

Take the responsibility for knowing what is happening around you.

Getting Good Visual Information

Your first line of defense is your eyes. Although good vision alone is no guarantee for defense, it is the principal input to your body's computer, the brain.

Studies indicate that 90% of your impressions of the driving scene are visual. To focus on a specific event or item in traffic, you have to rely on your central vision, which is a cone measuring only 3 degrees in width in the central part of your sight. Central vision is used for such things as estimating distance and reading details in the traffic scene.

Peripheral vision, although not as sharp as central vision, is more sensitive to light and movement than central vision is. It helps you detect important information coming into the traffic scene, even though you are not looking directly at such objects.

Visual Cues and Eye Movement

What visual cues do you actually use in driving? Vision research at the Ohio State University answered this question by devising a method to describe a vehicle operator's visual search process. This was done using an eye-movement recording system that showed where the motorist was looking while driving along the highway.

The recording system allowed researchers to document eye-movement patterns. They determined that inexperienced operators have an active search pattern with many fixations on unimportant clues. With experience, this progresses to an in-out pattern, sharing fixations for near lane position with glances ahead. The pattern exhibited by experienced riders is more desirable and effective.

Learning Good Eye Habits

The ultimate goal in eye movements while operating a motorcycle would be a pattern of far-ahead fixations in the projected path of travel, using side vision to maintain lateral positioning. Since this pattern is essential for valid perception, the question becomes, "How do you develop good eye habits?" There are at least three concepts that are critical to developing good eye habits:

1. Concentrate (focus) on your intended path of travel and move in traffic while maintaining adequate margins in all directions.

2. Aim your vision well ahead by keeping your eyes up.

3. Force your eyes to move frequently so that you receive a wide field of information.

In the ideal visual search process, the eyes function in a series of rapid, jerky movements. They fixate ever so briefly in between the movements. These fixations are rapid and last only between one-tenth and three-tenths of a second.

The eyes gather visual information during these brief fixations.

Bad Effects on the Visual Search Process

Physical limitations adversely affect this visual search process:

1. Fatigued operators tend to fixate lower and to the right, thus limiting their vision to only a small portion of the overall scene.

2. Alcohol-impaired operators fixate straight ahead and don't move their eyes often. Accident data indicates that alcohol is a contributing factor in at least 50% of the motorcycle-accident fatalities.

These limitations degrade your ability to see potential hazards, which can result in taking higher risks. Getting good visual information is critical for riders because everything that follows involves decisions based on that information. The key is to practice moving your eyes quickly and frequently to gather information. Knowing what is critical requires good judgment based upon knowledge and skill.

Visual Perception—What Is It?

Riding a motorcycle involves several rather complex functions. One of those functions is identifying critical cues in the traffic environment. This occurs in the **search** part of the mental system and depends on clear, accurate visual perception.

Visual perception is an active process in which we must purposely participate in order to make it work accurately. Perception calls upon senses (mostly sight in riding a motorcycle) for input to the brain. The brain processes the information to make it meaningful. Technically, visual perception is making sense of the many visual stimuli you receive.

When traffic is light, weather conditions good, and visibility and space favorable, all that's necessary is to choose a clear path and guide your motorcycle along it. Practically anyone can accomplish that. It's when things get hectic that the challenge increases. Decisions become more critical and a mistake more costly. Since decisions are all made based on perception, it is extremely important to attach the *correct* meaning to what is observed.

Delayed recognition or inaccurate perception of impending hazards starts a process that leads to bad decisions and inappropriate responses, which can end in a collision or other harmful event.

Eye control is fundamental to riding a motorcycle. *The machine will go where your eyes lead you.* The obvious point to be made is—look where you want to go. It sounds trite and simple to even mention such a ridiculously basic premise. However, thinking that this visual concept is simple and easy can be a drastic mistake. It isn't easy to actually do.

Sizing up your entry to a corner, then focusing on the small piece of roadway that represents your chosen apex, and finally swinging your eyes to the area of the exit where you will soon be, is all much more difficult than it sounds. Getting good at being able to concentrate your focus is directly related to the amount of practice applied. It's like perception—you aren't born with it, you must practice.

Good, dynamic eye habits properly focused reduces the likelihood of being lulled into **target fixation.** That's the term generally associated with staring at an area or object to such an extent that it draws you to it. You run over the object you most want to avoid or you cross the area in a turn that takes you off your line. For instance, fixating on the edge of the roadway instead of on your intended path can take you onto that edge and trouble. Concentrate on the path you intend to take. Looking at the area you intend to follow not only contributes to a smooth negotiation of the curve, but you also pick up any road-surface condition that may require an adjustment of your line. When your eyes negotiate a smooth curve, the rider and machine follow the same path.

Vision: Making the Most of It

We cannot effectively use any mental system without good vision or the ability to provide meaning to what we see. It may seem too obvious, but our first step is making sure we get the most from our sight. Let's review some things that can reduce our ability to see:

Inadequate Eye Protection
- Wind could cause watering
- Foreign objects could fly into eye

Alcohol and Other Drugs
- Tunnel vision
- Not able to focus
- Reduced low-light vision

Age
- Responsive focusing, near and far
- Inability to distinguish color

Environment
- Night
- Fog
- Glare
- Rain

Also, be sure to remove your sunglasses when riding through tunnels or other low-light areas. ■

Many riders think of the lane as being separated into thirds. Which position you choose depends on where other vehicles are, increasing your visibility, and avoiding hazards.

Positioning

Where you place yourself in the flow of traffic is another of your street-riding strategies. Position your motorcycle to create a "space cushion" between yourself and other vehicles. This not only helps you see traffic situations more clearly, it provides essential reaction time and leaves an escape route—an alternate path of travel.

Lane Placement

There is no one best lane position. You must constantly adjust and readjust your position depending on changing traffic conditions. These considerations affect your choice of lane position:

- Increasing your ability to see traffic.
- Increasing your visibility to other motorists.
- Avoiding other motorists' blind spots.
- Avoiding surface hazards.
- Protecting your lane from other drivers.
- Communicating your intentions.
- Avoiding wind blast from other vehicles.
- Providing an escape route.

Following Distance

A minimum space cushion allows two seconds between yourself, the car in front, and the car behind. Use a fixed-object count-off method to establish that following distance.

Pick out a fixed object, such as a street sign or light pole, ahead of you. As soon as the vehicle in front of you passes the object, count off, "One-thousand-one, One-thousand-two." If you haven't reached the same object by the time you finish counting, your following distance meets the two-second minimum for low speeds. But remember the word "minimum."

A safe following distance is based in part on a rider's ability to brake and the distance needed to stop. Looking ahead 12 to 14 seconds and actively scanning a four-second immediate path of travel will help you identify hazards that would require quick action.

Think of following distance as creating space in front of you in which to maneuver—space to swerve, brake, or a combination of both.

Following distance is not considered space for braking to a stop. You'll need more room (for time and distance) to brake to a stop.

Stopping Distance

When choosing a following distance, it is important to know that as speed increases, the distance required to stop increases dramatically. It is also important to recognize that it takes time to react before braking begins. That time translates into distance traveled.

Poor road conditions will increase the distance required to stop. Be prepared for longer stopping distances when stopping safely on wet roadways, or on loose or slippery roadway surfaces.

To be able to achieve maximum braking performance in real traffic situations, riders should:

- Actively search for potential hazards.
- Cover the brakes by lightly resting two or four fingers on the front-brake lever in high-risk areas. These include intersections, unfamiliar areas, and other traffic situations that would require quick stops. This will help minimize reaction time.
- Check traffic to the rear.
- Practice stopping quickly.
- Match following distances to stopping distances, especially at higher traffic speeds.

Learning to Use SIPDE

SIPDE is an acronym for the mental process we use to make judgments and take action in traffic. It stands for:

- **S**can
- **I**dentify
- **P**redict
- **D**ecide
- **E**xecute

Let's examine each of these steps.

Scan

Search aggressively for potential hazards. Scanning provides the information you need to make decisions and take action. Use the techniques for

The Effect of Speed on What We See

Speed is a critical factor in terms of our riding environment, vision, and managing time and space.

Imagine riding down your favorite country road at 25 miles per hour (40 KPH). Now imagine riding down the same road at 55 miles per hour (88 KPH). As our speed increases, we are approaching hazards at an increased rate. We might "see" a potential problem at the same distance. But seeing the problem is only one part of the process. Think about the time it may take for our minds to compare this with other problems. We need to assess the criticality and to weigh the options of what we might do. With training, knowledge, and background as experienced riders we probably can process this information quite quickly. But as speed increases, processing information becomes more critical.

One additional thought. Consider this situation. On your rural road, approximately 12 seconds ahead in your visual lead, are a parked car complete with driver, engine running, and a group of kids playing ball well off to the side of the road. The car is the major hazard that gets most of your attention. But as you approach, the game ball is kicked toward the road and the kids are not far behind. Your priorities may change. The higher your speed, the less time you may have to react.

No matter what the situation, your ability to place meaning in what you see becomes more critical with increased speed. ■

scanning that were discussed earlier in this chapter.

Identify

Locate hazards and potential conflicts. The hazards you encounter can be divided into three groups based on how critical their effect on you may be.

- **Cars, trucks, and other vehicles**—They share the road with you, they move quickly, and your reactions to them are critical.
- **Pedestrians and animals**—They are characterized by unpredictability and short, quick moves.
- **Stationary objects**—Chuckholes, guard rails, bridges, roadway signs, hedges, or rows of trees won't move into your path, but may create or complicate situations.

The greatest potential for a conflict between you and other traffic is at intersections. An intersection can be in the middle of an urban area or at a driveway on a residential street—anywhere other traffic may cross your path of travel. Most motorcycle/automobile collisions occur at intersections. And most of these collisions are caused by an oncoming vehicle turning left into the path of the motorcycle. Using SIPDE at intersections is critical.

Before you enter an intersection, scan for:

- Oncoming traffic that may turn left in front of you.
- Traffic from the left.
- Traffic from the right.
- Traffic approaching from behind.

Be especially alert at intersections with limited visibility. Be aware of visually "busy" surroundings that could camouflage you and your motorcycle.

Predict

Anticipate what the hazard might do. The direction of a potential hazard is important. Clearly, a vehicle moving away from you is not as critical as a vehicle moving in your path.

Determine what the hazard might do; where a collision might occur. How critical is the hazard?

How probable is a collision? Is there a need to downshift to be able to respond more quickly? This is the "What if . . ." phase of SIPDE that depends on your knowledge and experience. You must then estimate the consequences of the hazard. How might the hazard—or your effort to avoid it—affect you and others?

Decide

Determine what you need to do based on your prediction.

The mental process of determining your course of action depends on how aggressively you searched. The result is your action and knowing which strategy is best for the situation. You want to eliminate or reduce the potential hazard. You must decide when, where and how to take action. Your constant decision-making tasks must stay sharp to cope with constantly changing traffic situations.

The decisions you make can be grouped by the three types of hazards you encounter:

- **Single hazard**—This situation presents the most basic of decisions. Adjust speed and/or position to create more space and *minimize* the hazard.
- **Two hazards**—Apply the old adage, "One step at a time." Adjust your speed to permit the two hazards to *separate*. Then deal with them one at a time as single hazards.
- **Multiple hazards**—Sometimes two hazards won't separate. Sometimes you will be faced with more than two hazards. This is where decision-making becomes complex. You must weigh the consequences of the various hazards and *compromise* by giving equal distance to the hazards.

Execute

Carry out your decision. This is when your riding skills come into play. And this is where they must be second nature. The best decision will be meaningless without the skills to carry it out.

You carry out your decision in three ways:

1. **Communication** is the most passive action you can take since it depends on the response of someone else. Use your lights and horn, but don't rely on the actions of others.

2. **Adjust speed** by accelerating, slowing, or stopping.

3. **Adjust position** by changing lane position or completely changing direction.

The degree of adjustment depends on how critical the hazard is and how much time and space you have. The more time and space, the less the degree of adjustment, the less the amount of risk.

In areas of high potential risk, such as intersections, give yourself more space and take steps to reduce the time you need to react. Cover both brakes and the clutch and be ready with possible escape routes.

In fact, the greatest risk to all motorcyclists is the violation of their right-of-way by the driver of another vehicle. This occurs most often at intersections when a car turns left in front of the motorcyclist. You should be extra alert in such situations.

This is not to suggest that other hazards are not important, but the Hurt Study reported that "the failure of motorists to detect and recognize motorcycles in traffic is the predominating cause of motorcycle accidents. The driver of the other vehicle involved in a collision with the motorcycle did not see the motorcycle before the collision, or did not see the motorcycle until too late to avoid the collision."

One-third of all intersection accidents involve car drivers turning in front of other drivers and reporting that they didn't see the other car. The incidence of such accident configurations is higher for motorcyclists.

Detection Problems
Why does this happen more often with motorcyclists? There is no clear-cut answer. But there are many theories. We know that the problem centers on at least three potential factors:

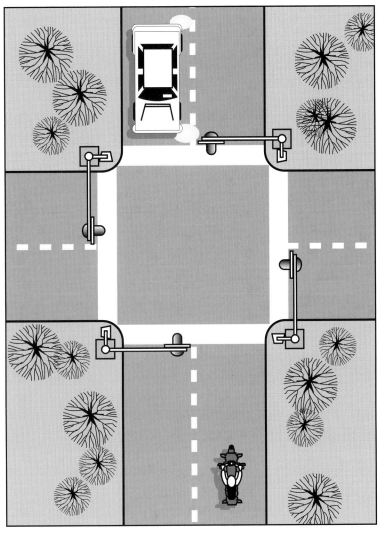

When faced with a single hazard, adjust speed and/or position to create more space and minimize the hazard.

1. **Detection of the motorcyclist** – People truly fail to detect a motorcycle in the traffic environment.

2. **Human visual-perception limitations** – People fail to attach valid, meaningful relationships to what they observe. Their matching, comparing, and association of the information they gather yields inaccurate conclusions.

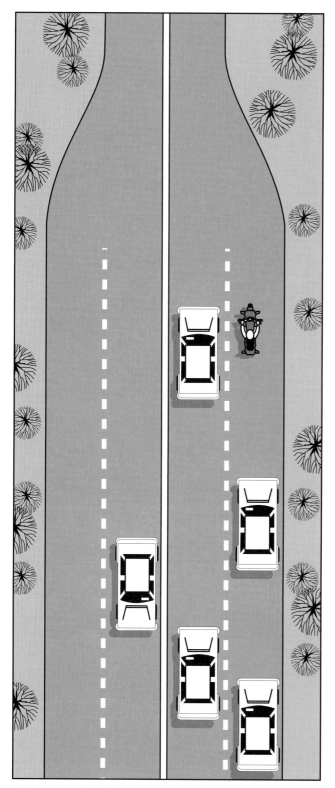

With two hazards, adjust your speed to permit them to separate. Then deal with them one at a time.

3. **Association** – The observer sees a motorcycle, then identifies it in the same category as a bicycle or moped. The motorcycle isn't viewed as a safety threat.

Suggested Treatments

The reason car drivers turn in front of motorcyclists more often than they do other vehicles may be caused by their judgment of the speed of the approaching motorcycle and the amount of space between their vehicle and the motorcycle.

A research study conducted by the University of Michigan developed some detectability treatments for both the motorcyclist and the motorcycle. Some of the more promising ones were tested in a study funded by the National Highway Traffic Safety Administration in 1978-79. The study, "Effects of Motorcycle and Motorcyclists' Conspicuity on Driver Behavior," found three treatments to be quite effective:

1. Headlights on.

2. High-visibility fabric for the rider's upper torso and a brightly colored helmet.

3. Modulation of the motorcycle headlight.

These treatments are not listed in degree of their importance. None of the three were found to be more effective than the others.

No one is sure what role failure to observe plays in this issue, but capturing the attention of those drivers who otherwise wouldn't see you is an important objective. To even stand a chance that they won't turn in front of you, you first have to be detected. Consider high-visibility upper torso clothing, a colorful helmet, and a headlight modulator. This is not to suggest that these items are "cure-alls" for the problem, but they proved beneficial in a scientific research project and, combined with other strategies, can be effective survival tactics.

Motorcyclists are ultimately responsible for their own well-being in traffic. It helps to know that the most prominent overall characteristic of multi-vehicle accidents (involving a motorcycle) is that a vehicle violates the motorcyclist's right-of-way more than half the time! Information and

If you can't separate multiple hazards, you must weigh the consequences of each one and compromise by giving equal distance to the hazards.

detection devices can help riders manage situations and aid their survival in traffic. So can an understanding of timing, positioning, and the use of space. Ride defensively. Wise motorcyclists use a strategy of assuming that they are invisible to other vehicle operators, even in broad daylight.

Now that we understand SIPDE and its importance, let's apply it to some of the common situations you'll face on the street.

Self-Test for Chapter 7:
Street Strategies and the Visual Edge

Choose the best answer to each question.

1. What is the most important part of any riding strategy?

    a. Speed.
    b. Maneuverability.
    c. Visibility.
    d. Riding ability.

2. How far down the road should you scan for potential hazards?

    a. 2 to 4 seconds ahead.
    b. 5 to 7 seconds ahead.
    c. 8 to 11 seconds ahead.
    d. At least 12 seconds ahead.

3. What is the minimum distance to maintain when following another vehicle?

    a. 2 seconds.
    b. 2 car lengths.
    c. 2 yards (1.8 meters).
    d. 20 feet (6 meters).

4. Where is the greatest potential for conflict between you and other traffic?

    a. Two-lane highway.
    b. Freeway.
    c. Residential street.
    d. Intersection.

5. Of the following, which is the greatest risk to all motorcyclists?

    a. Mechanical failure.
    b. Violation of their right-of-way by another vehicle.
    c. Oil on the road.
    d. Riding without a helmet.

(Answers appear on page 176.)

Looking In All Directions

Research tells us that the majority of the problems we face as riders are directly in front of us. However, it is also important to maintain our visual lead to the sides and to the rear.

We have defined "visual acuity" as the ability to provide meaning to what we see. The part of your vision with the greatest capability for visual acuity is in the center. This small demonstration should illustrate this point. You will need a piece of paper with some writing, picture, or diagram.

Look straight ahead. Hold the paper at about 90 degrees to one side at arm's length. While looking ahead, you probably can't read the writing or identify the picture. Rotate your arms and the paper forward until you can read the writing. Your ability to read the words increases as the paper gets closer to the center of your vision.

Notice, however, that you are able to detect the paper, even though you can't read the writing.

Let's return to our imaginary road, and again set our speed at 25 miles per hour (40 KPH). At lower speeds, we need to gather increased information from the sides. Consider what we discussed about our visual acuity. At lower speeds, we need to consciously **look** to the sides more often then we would at higher speeds. Things from the side can be a greater hazard at lower speeds. That dog sitting several hundred feet to the side of our path is a greater hazard at 25 MPH than at 55 MPH—he's more likely to catch us! At higher speeds, we will have seen the problem from a distance, made our decision, and taken whatever action was necessary long before we arrive. Of course, this again shows us that visual acuity is more important with increased speed.

Here's another interesting factor: As speed increases, our window of focus becomes smaller. One of the most graphic illustrations of this effect is on a roller coaster, which offers high speed and the close proximity of a super-structure. Next time you ride, note what happens to your side vision as the speed increases. Everything to the sides can quickly become blurred. ■

Applying Street Strategies

8

Where do you think most motorcycle accidents occur? It might seem to be on the freeway or on twisty mountain roads, but that isn't the case. According to the 1980 *Motorcycle Accident Cause Factors and Identification of Counter-measures* (the Hurt Study), the vast majority of motorcycle accidents occur on city streets. Ninety percent of all motorcycle accidents occur in the city or suburbs. And 74% are collisions with other vehicles, mostly passenger cars. So avoiding accidents is primarily a matter of knowing how to avoid collisions with cars.

In this chapter, we'll analyze several typical urban accident situations and examine ways that you can use SIPDE to avoid them.

The Shark

You are riding down a wide arterial street and observe a car moving up close behind you. The car tailgates for several blocks, and you decide to move out of the way. Just as you move into the other lane, the tailgater also changes lanes. What can you do to avoid a crash?

Strategy: When you observed the tailgater, you should have taken steps to move out of the way sooner. You could have signaled and pulled off to the right, or made a very obvious and gradual lane change to the left. When moving away from such "sharks," signal early and make definite moves so that the driver is fully aware of what you are doing.

The Shark

The Creeper

Riding a suburban street, you come up behind a slow-moving car. You would like to pass, but the driver keeps speeding up and slowing down, so you delay passing. After several blocks, you are frustrated by the slow pace and decide to accelerate past the car. Just as you pull out to pass the creeper, the driver makes a sudden left turn into a driveway. There's no room to stop or swerve.

Strategy: The car's erratic pace should have warned you that the driver was looking for something, possibly a street address, and was not observing the traffic following him. You should have predicted that the driver might turn or stop suddenly, and you should have decided to separate yourself from this hazard. You could have dropped back at least two seconds. You should never pass at an intersection or any other location where the car could make a turn in front of you.

Off-Ramp Dodger

You are riding on a downtown section of freeway, in the far right lane. Just as you are about to pass an off-ramp, a car in the lane to your left darts across your path and brakes hard to make the exit. You have no room to brake and a crash may be imminent.

Strategy: You could have observed the off-ramp approaching, and should have predicted that cars around you would exit. Since you are riding in the exit lane, drivers may assume you are going to ride off the exit, too. Knowing that off-ramps and on-ramps are prime locations for collisions, you should have decided to move away from the exit lane. And it is never a good tactic to allow yourself to ride in the blind spots of cars around you.

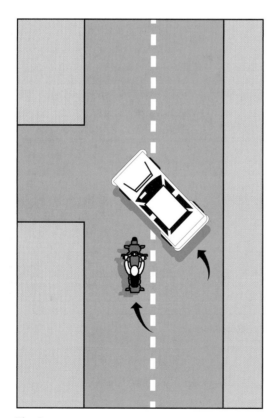

The Creeper

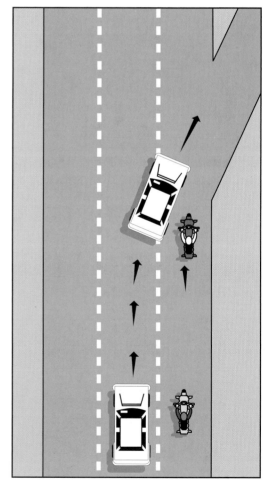

Off-Ramp Dodger

The Lane Changer

While riding in the right lane of a three-lane highway, you decide to pass a slower-moving car ahead by changing lanes to the left. Just as you change lanes, a car in the far left lane also decides to pass by moving to the right.

Strategy: Whenever changing lanes, position yourself so that you will still have road space after the change. You should have observed the car two lanes over, and predicted that the driver might also wish to change lanes to pass slower traffic. You could have decided to wait a moment before moving, or you could have dropped back one car length to avoid a possible collision. It is also a wise tactic to signal at least three seconds before the move, and to turn your head to observe surrounding traffic.

The Rear-Ender

Riding down a suburban street on a Saturday evening, you stop for a red light. Suddenly you hear the screech of tires, then a hard impact from behind knocks you out into the intersection. You have been struck by a car that didn't see you waiting for the light. The driver is drunk.

Strategy: Motorcycles can be difficult to see, especially at night. You should have predicted that a following driver might not see you, and scanned the rear-view mirrors for approaching traffic. Had you observed the fast-moving car approaching from behind, you could have quickly moved to one side to avoid a possible collision. It is not a wise practice to sit on a motorcycle in neutral in traffic. This is especially hazardous at night.

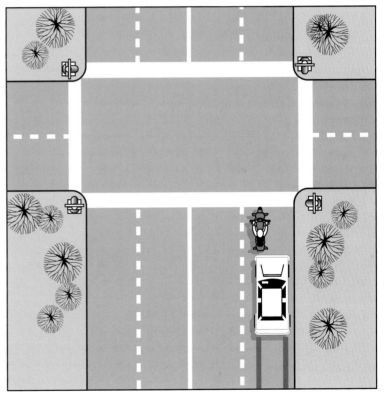

The Rear Ender

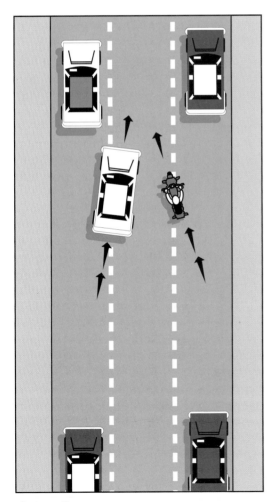

The Lane Changer

The Sleepy Commuter

On the way to work early one morning, you ride by a series of houses with cars parked in their driveways. Suddenly, one of the cars begins to move, and it backs right out into your path.

Strategy: You should have predicted that people would be leaving home for work at this hour, and that many of the cars would be backing out of driveways. You might have observed a driver getting into the car ahead, or noticed a puff of exhaust smoke as the car was started. You should have slowed and been prepared to stop quickly by covering the front brake lever. If there just wasn't room or time to stop, you might swerve to avoid the collision. The swerve could have been to the left if there was no oncoming traffic, or into the parking strip the car was vacating, then stop.

Considering that the majority of motorcycle accidents are collisions with passenger cars at urban intersections, you should know all you can about how and where such accidents occur. Examine some of these typical urban collisions.

The Basic Left-Turner

Approaching a four-way intersection along a busy arterial street, you are aware that cross traffic might not stop for the light, and that pedestrians might step out against the signal. There are cars waiting to turn. Just as you arrive at the intersection, the car in the opposing left turn lane jumps the light and swerves into your path.

Strategy: Although there are many potential hazards at the intersection, the left-turning car is your major concern. *The most frequent of all motorcycle/automobile accidents are collisions with left-turners.* You should predict that the car ahead might turn left in front of you, and reduce speed by shifting down and applying a little front brake. Slowing just 10 MPH (16 KPH) reduces your stopping distance almost by half, and covering the brake lever reduces the reaction time. Once you've slowed, keep an eye on the car in case you have to change position or stop quickly.

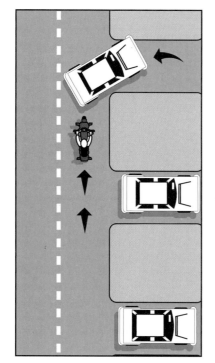

The Sleepy Commuter

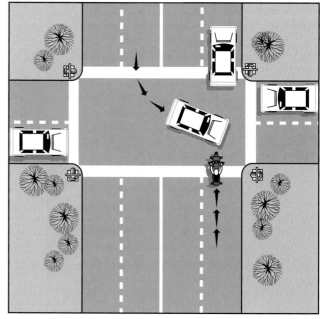

The Basic Left-Turner

The Hidden Left-Turner

You are riding in heavy traffic, following a bus. The bus enters an intersection. Suddenly a car appears in front of you, making a quick turn to pass behind the bus.

Strategy: This accident scenario is just like the first one, except the bus was blocking your view, and also blocking the left-turning driver's view of you. You should have predicted that a driver would try to slip through behind the bus. It is never wise to follow closely behind a large vehicle; you should have decided to move back where you could see and be seen.

Cars Waiting to Pull Out

You are riding along a wide arterial street, with a good view of traffic ahead. You observe a car waiting to pull out of a shopping center, but you have eye contact with the driver, and the car is not moving. Just as you are about to pass the shopping center exit, the driver accelerates out into your path, then jams on the brakes.

Strategy: Although you may realize that the majority of collisions occur at intersections, you may not know that one-third of motorcycle accidents occur on urban streets between intersections. Drivers waiting to pull out onto the street may not perceive a moving motorcycle, even if they appear to be looking directly at you. And, even if they do see you, they may not accurately judge your approach speed. You should be prepared to take evasive action to avoid any vehicle that could pull out into your path. As you approach, watch the front tire, which will provide the first indication that the car is starting to move. You can also help drivers to see you by wearing brightly colored clothing, and using the high beam during the daytime.

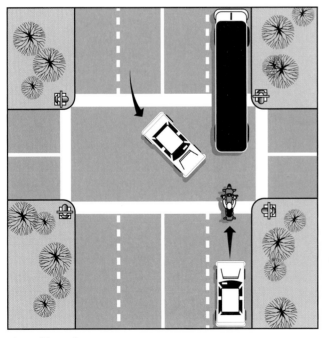

The Hidden Left-Turner

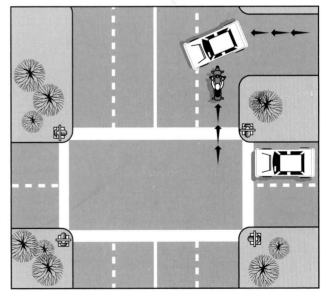

Cars Waiting to Pull Out

The One-Way Street

You are riding in the left lane of a one-way street, with a car ahead of you to your right. As the two of you enter an intersection, the car suddenly swerves left across your path to turn up a side street.

Strategy: Because traffic was light, the driver forgot the street was one-way, and did not look for you in his blind spot. Since there was no traffic approaching in the other lane, he felt free to make a normal left turn. You might not have predicted that this driver would turn left, but you should have predicted that all intersections are danger zones, and taken steps to separate yourself from the other vehicle. By riding in the driver's "blind spot," you effectively hide yourself.

Survival in traffic requires that you observe carefully what is happening, predict accurately what is about to happen, decide correctly how to deal with the hazards, and know how to control your motorcycle with the skill to make the right maneuver.

Here are some examples of how to apply the SIPDE approach to common street strategies. *Remember that these are examples and not universal solutions.* Every situation you encounter while riding will be different and require its own application of your street strategies. The important task is to apply the system that can help you execute good decisions.

Intersections

Scan a multi-lane controlled intersection with moderate moving traffic.

Identify a left-turning vehicle.

Predict that the driver does not see you and may turn left across your path.

Decide to brake then change lane position to increase gap and create room and time for turning vehicle.

Execute by applying both brakes smoothly to slow down—and move to the right portion of your lane. Continue SIPDE process.

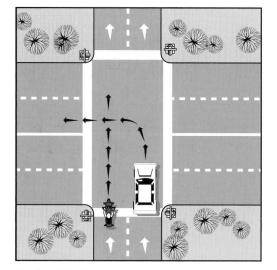

The One-Way Street

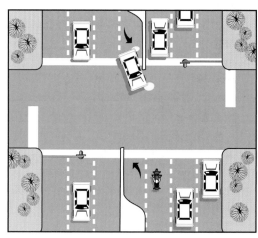

Intersection

Urban Multiple Intersections

Scan the two-lane roadway with multiple intersections or commercial entrances.

Identify the oncoming vehicle and unknown traffic at commercial entrances as two separate hazards.

Predict that the oncoming vehicle may turn left, and vehicles may enter from the driveways on the right.

Decide (separate) to adjust space and time by moving to the center portion of the lane to create space from the oncoming vehicle, and by slowing down. Prepare for further action.

Execute by using the throttle and brakes to adjust speed, steer to adjust position, cover brakes, and clutch. Continue SIPDE.

Urban Multiple Intersections

Merge Lane

Scan the two-lane roadway with merge lane and traffic to both sides.

Identify a vehicle entering from the right.

Predict that the vehicle on the right will enter the lane as you and the adjacent vehicle arrive at the point of the intersection.

Decide (separate) to create space to the front and sides. Slow and permit merging vehicle to enter. Allow the adjacent vehicle to pass.

Execute by applying both brakes smoothly. Check for vehicles behind and continue SIPDE.

Merge Lanes

Curved Road

Curved Road

Scan the curved mountain road with reduced visibility ahead.

Identify that there may be unknown hazards ahead. You are not able to see 12 to 14 seconds ahead. Visibility is limited to a four-second immediate path of travel.

Predict that unknown hazards will enter the path of travel with other unknown risks ahead.

Decide (minimize) to increase space and time to react, if necessary. Slow down.

Execute by rolling off the throttle and using your brakes to reduce speed and increase visibility as much as possible. Remain in the center lane position to permit increased cushion to oncoming vehicles. Continue SIPDE.

Multi-Lane Road

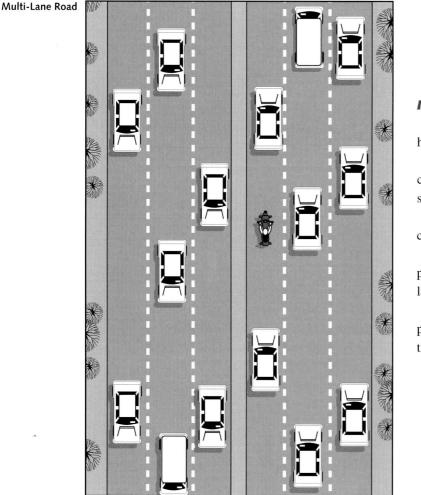

Multi-Lane Road

Scan the multi-lane divided highway with heavy traffic and reduced following distances.

Identify the other vehicles, reduced space cushion, inadequate following distance, reduced space to sides.

Predict that the vehicle to the right will change lanes into your space.

Decide (compromise) to communicate and protect your lane by moving to center third of lane. Prepare to take additional action.

Execute by using your horn. Steer to adjust position. Cover your brakes and clutch. Continue SIPDE.

Blind Hill

Scan the two-lane roadway with hills.

Identify that the hills reduce your 12-second visual lead with unknown hazards ahead.

Predict that an unknown hazard ahead will enter your path of travel (car crossing center lane) with additional unknown risk ahead.

Decide (minimize) to adjust space and time to react by reducing speed and moving to the center of your lane.

Execute by rolling off the throttle to adjust speed. Steer to adjust lane position and continue SIPDE.

Blind Hill

Passing Other Vehicles

Passing another vehicle with a motorcycle is not much different than passing with a car. However, visibility is more critical. Be sure other drivers see you.

- Ride in the left portion of the lane at a safe following distance. This position will increase your line of sight and make you more visible.
- Signal and check for oncoming traffic.
- Use your mirrors and make a headcheck to look for traffic approaching from behind.
- Move into the left lane and accelerate. Select a lane position that doesn't crowd the car you are passing and provides you with space to avoid possible hazards in the lane.
- Signal. Use your mirrors and make a headcheck to be sure you won't cut off the car you passed.
- Return to your lane.

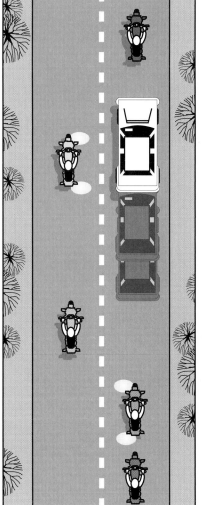

Passing Other Vehicles

Tailgaters

Another car may, for whatever reason, tailgate you. Identify that the tailgater does not have an adequate following distance. Predict that you may need to brake hard and that the vehicle behind you may not have enough room in which to perform hard braking. Decide that you must create more space between you and the tailgater.

Some options that you can execute are:

- Flash your brake lights to alert the tailgater.

- Gradually reduce your speed so that you have more space to the front.

- Maintain a lane position that discourages the tailgater from pulling up and sharing your lane, making the situation an even greater risk.

- Make a right turn at an intersection, if available, or pull well off the roadway to allow the tailgater to go around you and on his way.

Where Should Your Attention Be?

As you ride your motorcycle, where should your attention be? It makes sense to consider what direction most hazards come from.

Let's assume that, theoretically, a motorcyclist has 360 degrees of sight. For the sake of ease, let's turn this 360-degree circle into a clock face, with 12 possible positions ("hours").

Three researchers from the University of Southern California—Harry Hurt, James Ouellet, and David Thom—studied over 900 motorcycle accidents in the late '70s. Their findings were reported in *Motorcycle Accident Cause Factors and Identification of Countermeasures,* which was published in 1981.

In reconstructing those 900 accidents, the USC team determined the motorcyclist's line of sight to the other vehicle. For example, consider the motorcyclist approaching an intersection and an automobile in opposing traffic just beginning to turn left in front of the bike. The pre-crash line of sight would be approximately 11 o'clock.

As you can see by the diagram below, 77 percent of the crashes occurred in the 11-to-1 o'clock line of sight. The USC team said, "Motorcycle rider, watch where you are going; that is where at least three-fourths of the accidents are coming from!" (Of course, it's important to scan your mirrors, as stated on page 63, so that you have an "escape route" in case of vehicles violating your right-of-way. And it's vital to turn your head to look when changing lanes or turning.)

■

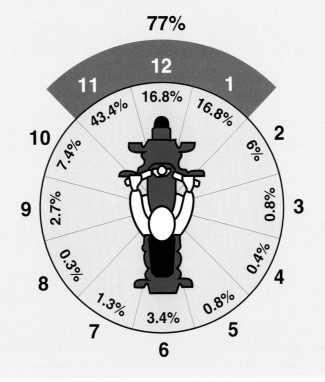

Cademartori

Special Situations

9

We live in an imperfect world. Sometimes that point is made all too clear when riding a motorcycle. Motorists often fail to see an oncoming motorcycle, dirt or debris can be in the middle of a blind corner, furniture can fall out of a truck, cars can break down in the middle of the road, or pedestrians can suddenly appear from behind a car. But with preparation, awareness, skill, and a little common sense, you can avoid the pitfalls of such common surprises. Here are some tips.

Maximum Braking

Stopping your motorcycle in the shortest possible distance is one of your most important skills because you never know when you'll need to use it.

The best way to achieve maximum braking is to apply both brakes fully without locking either wheel. Squeeze and apply steady pressure. Remember to keep the clutch pulled in as you downshift to first gear. Sit straight on the motorcycle and look well ahead—don't look down at the ground.

Controlling Skids

Situations can occur that may cause you to unintentionally lock a wheel and skid while braking. A front-wheel skid is difficult to control. Should it occur, release the front brake immediately.

Rear-wheel skids occur more commonly since, during braking, the weight of the motorcycle and rider is transferred away from the rear wheel and to the front. But a rear-wheel skid is not necessarily dangerous when you know how

to control it. On pavement, keep the rear wheel locked and skidding to avoid a "high-side" (being thrown from the motorcycle). Keep looking well ahead and steer the motorcycle to maintain a straight path of travel. Keep the motorcycle straight up—don't lean.

On loose surfaces, such as gravel, and at low speeds, ease off pressure from the rear brake to stop the skid. Again, keep looking well ahead and don't lean.

Stopping In a Curve

The important point to remember when stopping in a curve is that the amount of traction available for braking is reduced. There is a limited amount of force existing between your tires and the road. When turning, you are using up a portion of that force. The greater your lean angle, the more traction force you are using. The bottom line is that when you are turning, you have less traction available for braking. (See Chapters 10 and 11 for more on traction.)

The key to stopping in a curve is to get the motorcycle straight up as soon as possible so that the maximum amount of traction is available for braking. If road conditions permit, straighten the motorcycle quickly and "square" the handlebars as you apply the brakes. In effect, you are making a straight-line stop.

Conditions may not always permit you to straighten up the motorcycle, then stop. In such cases, apply the brakes smoothly, and gradually start slowing the motorcycle. As you slow down,

Always remember that traction is limited. If you must brake and swerve, separate the two.

knees snugly against the tank and your feet solidly on the pegs. Do not look at the object you're trying to avoid. Look at the path that will avoid it. Make your escape route the target for your vision.

Do not brake while swerving. Remember that traction is limited. If braking is required, separate it from swerving.

Surmounting Obstacles

A motorcycle is no match for a car or truck. Hitting most animals would also likely cause a crash. But there are some smaller obstacles that you can ride over. Potholes, speed bumps, wood pieces, tailpipes, and smaller bits of highway trash can be ridden over by standing on the pegs and using your legs to help absorb some of the shock.

First, you must determine if it is practical to go over the obstacle. Then approach the obstacle at as close to a 90-degree angle as possible. Control your path of travel by looking to where you want to go.

As you approach the object, rise slightly off the seat. Keep your knees bent and against the tank. Shift your weight to the rear and, if at low speed, roll on the throttle to lighten the front wheel and ride across the obstacle. When the front tire contacts the obstacle, roll off the throttle. As the rear wheel encounters the object, allow the rear of the bike to rise. Be prepared for the rear end to kick to one side. If this happens, open the throttle. Applying power will help straighten the bike when the rear wheel comes down.

you can reduce your lean angle and apply more brake pressure until the motorcycle is straight and maximum brake pressure is possible. In either case, remember that the motorcycle should be straight up when you come to a full stop. If you "square" the handlebar in the last few feet of stopping, you know the motorcycle will be straight up and in balance.

Evasive Maneuvers

Use evasive maneuvers to avoid situations where stopping isn't a reasonable solution. Basically, you have two choices: go around or go over.

Swerving

Swerving is two consecutive quick turns, one right after the other. You'll sometimes hear this referred to as "two consecutive countersteers." Remember that a motorcycle turns by leaning and that to lean the motorcycle, push on the handgrip in the direction of the turn. Push right—lean right—go right. Push left—lean left—go left.

To swerve to the left, push left then push right. To swerve to the right, push right then push left. Let the motorcycle move beneath you. It will react more quickly that way. Just keep your

Applying Evasive Maneuvers

Quick Lane Change

Swerve to avoid vehicles slowing or merging. You can also use this technique to avoid objects in the roadway.

Pedestrians

Usually brake first, then swerve into the space the pedestrian has left.

Because the situations described here are generalized and depend on the specific actions of others, you will have to determine the best action to take in the circumstances you face. Use your street-riding strategies. Use SIPDE.

Roadway Conditions

There are a number of things that can make roads more challenging for the motorcyclist. In fact, the road surface itself can be a problem. Here are just a few of the surface imperfections you may encounter:

- **Gravel roads** will reduce traction and give the motorcycle a "loose" feel. Reduce speed and don't abruptly change direction or speed.
- **Spills** of sand, gravel, fuel, oil, or coolant on the pavement will create slick spots. Use SIPDE to avoid them. If they can't be avoided, ride through at a constant speed. Make any speed and direction changes before reaching the slippery patch.
- **Rain grooves** will give your motorcycle a loose feel, but they don't reduce traction. Reduce speed as necessary to feel comfortable.
- **Bridge gratings** combine the loose feel of rain grooves with reduced traction, especially when wet. Slow before you reach them and avoid abrupt speed and direction changes once you're on them.
- **Bumps and cracks** are obstacles to ride over. If large enough, they may jar a motorcycle off its path. Cross them at as close to 90 degrees as possible, maintain a constant speed and, if necessary, rise off the seat as you go over them.

If you need to make a quick lane change—to avoid vehicles that are slowing or merging, or objects in the roadway—swerve with two quick countersteers (see Chapter 13).

- **Crowned roads** will limit your lean angle in left turns by reducing cornering clearance. Adjust speed accordingly.
- **Icy or extremely slick surfaces** (like mud, snow, or ice) squeeze the clutch and coast straight through.
- **Rain** also reduces your traction. Lower your speed and avoid any abrupt moves. The road surface is slickest during the first minutes of the rain before the dirt and oil are washed away. Try to avoid riding when the first drops begin falling.

Carrying Passengers

Carrying a passenger is a great way to share the joy of motorcycling . . . when it's done correctly. First you should adjust the suspension and tire pressures to allow for the additional weight of your passenger. Then be sure the passenger is dressed as well as you are—with a helmet and all proper riding gear.

Finally, review these basic rules with your passenger:

- Before climbing on the machine, the passenger should wait until the rider gets the bike off the stand and braced vertically.

- The passenger should grasp the rider's upper arm or shoulder when ready to get on, both as a signal and as a help in balancing. Then stand on the left footpeg or footboard with your left foot, swing your right leg over the saddle, and sit down, keeping body weight centered over the machine as well as possible. (Climbing off at the end of the ride is just the reverse.)
- Always hold onto the operator's waist or hips for stability. (You can also hold onto the seat strap or rail.)
- The passenger's feet stay on the pegs at all times, including while stopped.
- The passenger's hands and feet should be kept away from hot or moving parts.
- The motorcycle operator sits in front. Passengers should not try to control the motorcycle. When turning, they should look over the operator's shoulder in the direction of the turn. Otherwise, passengers should avoid leaning and making any unannounced shifts of weight.

As the operator, you have a few rules, too.

- The added weight of your passenger will affect turning and stopping. Get used to the differences in handling.
- Start the engine before your passenger gets on. Hold the front brake while your passenger mounts and dismounts.
- Don't try to impress your passenger with your skill and daring. For the new passenger, the best impression will be from a smooth, relaxed ride.

Carrying Other Loads

There are three points to consider when carrying loads on your motorcycle:
- How much the load weighs.
- Where the load is located.
- How the load is secured.

Weight

Every motorcycle has a maximum load capacity specified by its manufacturer. It is the difference between the empty weight and the maximum allowable weight of the motorcycle and all of its load, including the rider and passenger.

Before packing for a trip, subtract your weight (dressed in riding gear, not fresh out of the shower), your passenger's weight, about 30 pounds (13 kilograms) for a full tank of gas, and the empty weight of the motorcycle from its specified maximum weight. What you have left is the load you can carry.

However, you need to be aware of one more thing: saddlebags, tankbags, luggage racks, etc., have their own weight limits. Don't exceed them. Although you may be able to fit 50 pounds (22 kilograms) of roofing nails in a top trunk, if it is rated for only 20 pounds (9 kilograms), put no more than 20 pounds in it.

Windshields can increase your comfort, but they are an additional weight and can affect tire wear.

Finally, be sure to adjust tire pressures and suspension to handle the extra load. Refer to your owner's manual.

Location

Due to a motorcycle's size, weight, and the fact that it has two wheels, where a load is carried is important. Concentrate the weight low and to the center of the motorcycle. Keep the weight even, side to side, and try to place heavier items in the "load triangle" determined by your head and the two axles.

Although luggage racks and top trunks appear to be ideal places to pack things, carrying weight high and to the rear of the motorcycle will lighten the front wheel and may cause handling instability. Never strap things to the handlebar, front forks, or front fender. Even if handlebar and suspension travel is unaffected, the weight can cause steering instability.

Mounting

Be sure the load is secure. Use accessory racks and luggage designed for your specific motorcycle. Secure loose items with bungee cords and web straps. Don't block lights or moving suspension pieces. And be sure there are no loose items to blow about. Having a jacket chewed by the drive chain is hard on the jacket; but if it should jam and lock the rear wheel, it may be hard on you, too!

One more consideration is common sense. Regardless of weight, some things, like surfboards and sousaphones, just don't belong on motorcycles. When in doubt, leave it home.

Handling Special Situations

Tire Blowout

The most common cause of tire failure is underinflation. Check your tires frequently and keep them inflated to the manufacturer's specifications.

If a puncture should occur, keep a firm hold on the handlegrips. Steer smoothly and ease off the throttle. Avoid downshifting and braking. If traffic permits, slow gradually and move off to the side of the road. If you must brake, use the brake on the wheel with the good tire. Be aware that integrated braking systems don't allow for "rear brake only" application.

Broken Clutch Cable

It is possible, but not advisable, to shift gears without using the clutch. (Many riders have done this when they were learning to ride.) Just roll off the throttle and press hard on the shift lever. It will be a little jerky, but it works.

If you have a broken clutch cable, stopping smoothly is the problem—you only get one chance. If possible, travel to a place where help will be available. Downshift one gear at a time to first and stop the engine using the engine cut-off switch. The stop won't be smooth, so be prepared.

In traffic, the best solution is to ride to a safe spot by the side of the road as soon as possible.

Animals

Some dogs chase sticks, others chase motorcycles. If you encounter the motorcycle-chasing variety, you will probably see it approaching. Slow down until your paths are close, then accel-

Concentrate luggage weight low and to the center of the motorcycle (in the "load triangle" determined by your head and the two axles). Keep the weight even, side to side.

erate away. This will throw off the dog's planned point of interception and leave it frustrated.

Larger animals present larger problems. Wild animals, such as deer, are unpredictable. Be alert in wooded areas and be prepared to stop.

Avoiding smaller animals also presents problems, but keep one thing in mind: given the choice between hitting a rabbit and hitting a guard rail, there is only one rational decision.

Wind

A steady wind is not much of a problem. Just lean the motorcycle into it. If the wind is from the left, press on the left handgrip and the motorcycle will lean. Gusting winds require immediate reactions. Give yourself room to maneuver. Use SIPDE to predict where the wind will change: trucks, bridges, overpasses, and large buildings will create gusts.

Wobble/Weave

These are related but distinct handling problems usually caused by excessive weight in the wrong place or mechanical problems. A weave is an oscillation of the rear of the motorcycle while a wobble is a rapid shaking of the handlebar.

The difference is academic since the solution is the same. Keep a firm hold on the handlegrips but don't lock your arms and fight them. Ease off the throttle as you move your weight down and forward.

And don't believe the "old timers" who say to accelerate through a wobble. It doesn't work.

Parking

Without an engine to power it and a rider to guide it, a motorcycle is rather helpless. Keep these points in mind when you leave your motorcycle on its own:

- Park at an angle with the rear wheel to the curb (check local laws).

- If you leave your motorcycle on its sidestand, turn the handlebar to the left. In any case, lock the forks.

- The "feet" on side and centerstands will sink into soft surfaces. If they sink far enough, you'll return to find your motorcycle on its side. If you must park on a soft surface, use the sidestand and place a flat object, such as a flattened can, under the sidestand's foot.

Self-Test for Chapter 9:
Special Situations

Choose the best answer to each question.

1. What is the best way to achieve maximum braking?

    a. Use the front brake.
    b. Use the rear brake.
    c. Lock both brakes.
    d. Apply both brakes without locking the wheels.

2. When swerving to avoid an object, where should you be looking?

    a. At the object.
    b. At the path that allows you to avoid it.
    c. Up.
    d. Down.

3. Carrying a passenger . . .

    a. Affects the way your motorcycle handles and stops.
    b. Is forbidden in some states.
    c. Will cause you to crash.
    d. None of the above.

4. What is the best way to handle a tire blowout?

    a. Apply maximum braking.
    b. Swerve to the side of the road.
    c. Ease off the throttle and steer smoothly to the roadside, braking with the "good" wheel.
    d. Stand up to take the weight off of the wheels.

(Answers appear on page 176.)

Riding at Night . . .

There are times when you must continue riding at night, or times when you choose to go for a ride after the sun goes down. You may find yourself miles from home as it gets dark, or you may choose to ride at night to cross the desert and avoid the daytime heat. Whatever the reasons for riding at night, there are some special considerations for motorcyclists.

Vision is one of our most important considerations. If you can't see where you are going, you can't stay on the road. If you can't see the hazards ahead, you can't take evasive action. The human eye is not well adapted to nighttime vision, and it is sensitive to chemicals such as alcohol and carbon monoxide. Human eyes take several minutes to adjust chemically from very bright surroundings to dim light levels. Consider what happens when your photograph is taken with a flash. You are momentarily blinded until your eyes can adjust. The same thing happens when going from a brightly lit restaurant to a dark parking lot, or when you stare at the headlights of an oncoming vehicle. There are several tactics you can use to maximize your nighttime vision:

- Use only *clear* eye protection, and keep it clean and free of scratches.
- Avoid alcohol and smoking before or during a night ride.
- Wait a few moments after leaving a bright area before riding away. Allow your eyes time to adjust to the low light level.
- Practice *avoiding* bright light sources as you ride along. Look to one side of street lights, signs, or headlights. For example, as a car approaches, shift your vision from the headlights to the white line along the edge of your lane.

(continued)

When riding at night, remember that the human eye is sensitive to chemicals such as alcohol and carbon monoxide, and takes several minutes to adjust from very bright surroundings to dim light levels.

. . . Riding at Night . . .

Another consideration is protective gear. Since you can't always see the condition of the road surface, you are more likely to have a spill at night. And, since the air temperature usually drops significantly after dark, you also need more insulation. So night riding demands the best riding gear. A full-coverage helmet provides much better insulation and facial protection.

Fatigue is a common problem at night, especially on longer rides. It is easy to get weary while riding but procrastinate in taking a rest break. Yet failing to deal with fatigue can create a situation that leads to an accident. Smart riders take more frequent rest breaks at night. They get off the machine and do some exercises to get the blood flowing again. As a minimum, consider walking briskly to the other end of the parking lot and back. Coffee stops are beneficial, not only for the beverage, but also for the change of pace.

If you just can't seem to stay awake, find a suitable spot and take a short nap, or even stop at a motel and check in for some sleep. A room for the night is a lot cheaper than a crash.

Wild animals are more likely to be roaming the highway at night, especially during the spring and fall. Animals such as deer are difficult to see at night, and hitting a deer with a motorcycle can be disastrous for both animal and human. The correct tactic for avoiding a deer strike is to brake quickly to a slow speed when a deer is seen ahead. Deer eyes reflect light much as a glass reflector. If a "reflector" alongside the road winks off and on, it is very likely a deer or some other small animal. Remember that deer travel in families, so one deer indicates that others are nearby.

Of course, it helps to spot wild animals if your headlight is bright and aimed correctly. Your high beam should strike the road surface at its maximum range, yet allow the low beam to be below the eye level of approaching motorists to avoid blinding them. If you make frequent night-time trips, consider adding an auxiliary driving light, wired into the high-beam circuit. Remember, all vehicle lights must conform to the equipment laws of the state in which you are riding.

You will also help yourself to be more readily seen by adding reflectors or reflective tape to the rear panels of tail trunks and saddlebags, or adding extra taillights. The human eye has trouble judging the distance of red light, which may contribute to an increase in rear-end collisions at night. Reflective clothing and added lights can help other drivers to judge your distance.

When riding in traffic, try to maintain more space around you, and be especially wary of vehicles approaching from behind. Adjust your riding tactics to avoid having to stop in the middle of the street waiting for traffic signals. When approaching a stop signal, adjust speed so that you don't have to wait a long time for the light. When making a left turn, consider going around the block to the right, rather than waiting in the left turn lane where a sleepy driver could pick you off.

(continued)

. . . Riding at Night

You may decide to follow another vehicle at night to take advantage of the additional lights, or to help avoid animal strikes. By observing when the lights of the vehicle in front of you bounce up and down, you can get an idea of where potholes are. If you do follow a car or truck, increase your following distance to at least four seconds to allow space for braking. Make a point of counting out your following distance in seconds, rather than just guessing. When the car ahead passes by a stationary point such as a street light, start counting, "one-thousand-and-one, one-thousand-and-two . . ." If you can count to four before passing the same street light, you are at the minimum distance.

Be aware of other vehicles that seem to pace you at night. Some drivers are merely curious, but there are also "weirdos" looking for a little entertainment, and you could be the victim. Change speed or lanes to create space around you and separate yourself from possible problems. When pulling into rest areas or restaurant parking lots, scrutinize the night life there before shutting off the engine. If you don't like the looks of the place, move on, and find someplace more friendly.

Some riders enjoy night riding, some tolerate it occasionally, and some motorcyclists can't stand it at all. If you have reservations about night riding, or can't seem to keep your eyes open after dark, don't do it. ■

Raising a Fallen Bike . . .

Most of the time you manage to keep your motorcycle upright, but every now and then you may have to raise a machine that has toppled over. You're most likely to drop a bike at very slow speeds, or even when standing still. Perhaps you didn't really want to make a *complete* stop, just do a sort of "rolling" stop and keep going. But when that car suddenly changed lanes you did have to make a quick stop, and the bike toppled over before you could get your foot down. Or perhaps you merely stopped for a drink of water on a hot day, and came back to find the sidestand had sunk into the hot asphalt and permitted the machine to fall over.

Whatever the size of your bike, the trick to raising a fallen machine is to use leverage and avoid straining your back. You may be so embarrassed at dropping your bike that you quickly grab hold and attempt to wrestle it upright by brute force. Even a middleweight can cause injury if you don't pay attention to how you do it.

If the fallen machine has engine-protection bars, the technique is to grasp both handlebars, rock the bike *toward* you on the engine-protection bars, and use momentum to roll it back upright. Bend your knees, not your back, and use leg power to push the machine upright. If the bike has fallen on a slope, pivot it around so that it points uphill before attempting to raise it, and shift the transmission into first gear.

If your machine isn't equipped with engine-protection bars, you'll either have to get some additional muscle, or use leverage. If you're on your own, grasp the low handlebar, turn the front wheel toward you, grasp something solid along the frame, and work your knees up under the saddle to help lever the bike upright. Use your legs to push. If the machine has fallen on its right side, it's a good idea to extend the sidestand before raising it, just in case you lose your balance and can't keep it from falling the other way as you get it up.

When attempting to raise any machine, remember that gasoline may have spilled from the tank or carburetors. Not only is spilled fuel a fire hazard, it can also make the pavement very slippery. Avoid smoking near any fallen bike, and watch where you step when attempting to lift it. There are two other fluids that can spill and cause damage. Battery acid may leak from vent holes or fill caps while the machine is on its side. Acid can cause burns to skin, eat holes in your riding gear, and corrode the frame. After a spill, smart riders make a point of flushing the battery area with lots of water. Brake fluid won't burn your skin, but it can be disastrous for paint and plastic parts. Immediately wipe clean any spilled brake fluid and wash the area with soap and water as soon as possible.

(continued)

. . . Raising a Fallen Bike

Of course, your immediate concern after a spill is the cosmetic damage to paint, chrome, and plastic parts. But you should also be concerned with hidden damage that could cause serious problems as you ride away. Brake, clutch, and shift levers can be bent in a fall, and can subsequently fracture when you don't expect it. Sometimes you can straighten bent levers without cracking, but it is a wise precaution to replace any bent lever as soon as possible. It also makes sense to check the running gear after a fall, to be certain a fender isn't rubbing the tire, or that a brake cable or hose hasn't been damaged. If any brake fluid has been spilled, refill the fluid in the reservoir to prevent air from being pumped into the brake system. L kewise, check the battery electrolyte level.

Lessen the chances of dropping your bike by practicing some simple habits. First, whenever you climb on or off the bike, always squeeze the front brake lever to prevent the machine from rolling. Second, when you stop, make a *complete* stop, using lots of front brake. Riders who have to make several dabs with their foot while the bike creeps to an unpredictable stop are very likely to drop the machine.

Finally, park your bike sensibly. Point the front end uphill, even if you have to roll backward into a parking spot. If you can't lodge the rear wheel against a curb, leave the transmission in first gear. Be sure the bike leans over against the sidestand, so that it isn't likely to topple over the other way should someone bump it. And place something flat under the sidestand if the asphalt paving is hot, to prevent the stand from sinking. A small piece of metal such as a flattened can will help keep a sidestand from sinking when parking on grass or dirt.

Since it is more difficult to balance at slow speeds, you can reduce your chances of dropping your bike by practicing slow-speed maneuvers. If you haven't yet taken the *Experienced RiderCourse* (see Chapter 17), that's an excellent place to start your slow-speed practice. ∎

Group Riding

10

Few things on the road are more impressive than a large group of motorcyclists riding together in formation. People stop what they're doing to stare or wave, and children can't be pulled away until the last motorcycle disappears behind the ridge. It's a wonderful, goose-bumpy feeling to ride in a group. Smaller groups can provide added security, companionship, and additional resources to members on tour. As marvelous as group riding can be, it is equally unpleasant without preparation, organization, and consideration for others.

There are many different aspects to the topic of group riding, depending on your interest. Much has been written for organizers and leaders of group rides, often in conjunction with information about touring, rally organization, etc. The focus of this section is on you, the individual rider, as a participant in different types of group rides and how you can maximize your enjoyment of this social type of motorcycling.

We've already discussed many of the mental and physical skills involved in riding a motorcycle. Certainly these same skills come into play when riding in a group, but there are some differences as well. For example, when we discussed preparation we did not suggest taking into account anybody's needs but your own. When riding with a group, you don't always decide when to leave or where to go. The concepts of space cushioning and following distance have obvious applications when you are surrounded by other riders.

Group rides often consist of people with a wide variety of experience and skill. The pace and the expectations within the group should not be set higher than the limits of each individual's abilities and equipment. Less-seasoned riders may find themselves riding "way over their heads" in an effort to stay with the group, putting both themselves and others in jeopardy. Likewise, too slow a pace may frustrate or annoy riders who feel that they must stay within the group.

There are many types of group rides, each with a different set of characteristics, goals, and joys. A common one is the small, sometimes informal "touring group." You may have been out for a ride and met several other motorcyclists en route. Perhaps you "hit it off" and agreed to ride together for some distance. Or maybe you are a member of a group that gets together regularly to ride. These types of group rides often fall into one of two categories. **Destination-oriented rides** are focused on a goal. Plans may be made just for one direction with an event or place at the end. **Route-oriented rides** are more for the joy of motorcycling together. They may be scenic, closed-loop tours or explorations of new areas without a fixed timetable or plan.

Benefits and celebrations are often associated with group rides on a much grander scale. These can be money-raising events with lots of publicity. The image that the group projects is a significant part of the ride and has the potential to influence public opinion.

If you are riding in staggered formation, allow a full two seconds following distance between you and the rider directly in front of you. The leader rides in the left side of the lane, while the second rider stays one second behind in the right portion of the lane, and so on.

Poorly managed group rides can fall into a class by themselves. Occasionally a group participant might act competitive or "ego-oriented." If for any reason you find yourself in a group that you don't feel comfortable with, find a way to improve or remove yourself from the situation. Don't just press on, hoping that things will get better without your input.

Joining a group ride involves both physical and mental preparation. You are responsible for making sure that your motorcycle has a full gas tank and that you are ready to leave on time. Find out as much as possible about the route, purpose, and any other special requirements, such as tolls, rest/gas stops, escorts, etc. If the group uses signals to communicate, or a "buddy" system, make sure you understand and abide by the rules and protocol. Be certain that you know enough about the route to be able to leave the ride if the need arises.

Ideally, groups should not be too large—perhaps five or six motorcycles. Larger groups can break up into smaller ones that ride independently but near each other to achieve the benefits of a smaller group size. Too large a group may have difficulty in areas with traffic controls, obstruct through or surrounding traffic, and have difficulty adjusting their speed or direction in a coordinated fashion.

Riding in Formation

Several riding formations are popular, depending on the riding environment and group. **Staggered formations** allow a full two seconds following distance to be maintained between you and the rider directly in front of you without stretching the group out over a long distance. The leader rides in the left side of the lane, while the second rider stays one second behind in the right portion of the lane. A third rider maintains the left position in the lane, two seconds behind the first rider. The fourth rider would keep a two-second distance behind the second rider, and so on. This formation keeps the group close and permits each rider a safe distance from others ahead, behind, and to the sides. Increase your space cushion in inclement weather to avoid road spray and "rooster tails."

Single-file formations are more appropriate for twisty mountain roads where the group may need to spread out and use the entire width of the lane. Toll booths or certain highway-access points may require the use of a single-file formation.

Side-by-side formations generally leave a poor space cushion to the side, so they should generally be discouraged unless required by the circumstances. For example, an escort may require side-by-side riding within a group in areas of dense traffic to facilitate moving the group through quickly.

Keep the Group Together

If you are the leader of a group, look ahead for openings to make lane changes on highways. Signal early so those following have plenty of time to get the message and prepare for the maneuver. Start lane changes as early as practical to permit everyone to complete the change.

You should encourage inexperienced motorcyclists to ride toward the front of the group, where more seasoned riders who follow can watch them.

Let the tailender set the pace. Use your mirrors to keep an eye on the person behind you. If a rider falls back, slow down a little to prevent him or her from dropping too far behind. If everyone uses this technique, the group will be able to maintain a fairly steady speed without the need for others to "catch up."

Passing in Formation

Riders in a staggered formation should pass one at a time. First, the leader should pull out and pass when it is safe. After passing, the leader should return to the left position and continue riding at passing speed to open room for the next rider.

When the first rider passes safely, the second rider should move up to the left position and watch for a safe chance to pass. After passing, this rider should return to the right position and open up room for the next rider.

It is not a good idea for the leader to move to the right portion of the lane after passing a vehicle. It encourages the second rider to pass and cut back in before there is a large enough space cushion in front of the passed vehicle. It's simpler and safer to wait until there is enough room ahead of the passed vehicle to allow each rider to move into the same position held before the pass.

When it is time for the group to stop, try to stay in formation and wait your turn to park. One rider out of place can greatly disrupt the flow of traffic and create confusion for everyone. Ideally, you should try to avoid having to make left turns across traffic by choosing an open area on the right side of the road with ample space and easy access to stop. Don't wander too far unless you know when the group is planning on getting started again, or you may find yourself unintentionally riding alone!

Your preparation, skills, and rider responsibility—knowing your limits and the limits of the group and taking the responsibility to ride within them—is the key to making this social form of motorcycling fun for everyone. You may find that group riding is the most enjoyable type of riding for you.

Choose the best answer to each question.

1. Ideally, groups should consist of how many motorcycles?

    a. Two or three.
    b. Five or six.
    c. Ten to fifteen.
    d. Twenty to thirty.

2. There are three main types of riding formations. Which one is best for maintaining space between you and the rider in front of you, without stretching the entire group out over a long distance?

    a. Single-file formation.
    b. Side-by-side formation.
    c. Staggered formation.
    d. Rock formation.

3. Where is the best place to put an inexperienced rider?

    a. In front of the leader.
    b. Behind the leader.
    c. Second to the last.
    d. Last.

4. Your group is riding on a two-lane highway. As the leader, you carefully pass a car. Once you are in front of the car, you should move into the right portion of the lane to make room for the next rider. True or false?

(Answers appear on page 176.)

PART III

Go: Advanced Theory for Experienced Riders

Traction

11

What Is Traction?

No matter what your technical background is, or how much you understand physics, traction is important to you as a motorcyclist. Simply put, traction is the *grip* or the *potential for friction between your tires and the surface of the road.* Motorcycle tires can produce a lot of traction on clean, dry pavement. Have you ever tried to push a motorcycle on a flat surface while a rider was seated on it? It isn't that difficult if the motorcycle is in neutral and the rider doesn't touch either brake's control. If the rider is applying both brakes, the task becomes quite a bit harder! The difference is due to traction.

Motorcycles are designed to provide plenty of traction while riding in a straight line under ideal conditions, but the riding conditions are constantly changing and the road isn't always straight and level. Very few motorcyclists would have it any other way! Changes in the weather, road surface, camber, and direction are some of the things that make riding more enjoyable. However, all of these things also affect traction. Responsible motorcycling demands that a rider be aware of the traction available at all times to effectively manage its use.

Why Is Traction Important?

We have already discussed some of the mental skills involved in riding a motorcycle. The primary goal of using a mental riding strategy is to minimize the risks associated with the many hazards on the street. Experience and effective hazard management will reduce the demand on your physical skills by helping you to stay out of situations that require a dramatic response.

Even the most experienced rider cannot predict the future, and we all know that it is critical to be ready for the unexpected when riding. "Being ready" means having a plan, maintaining sharp, practiced physical riding skills, and having the means to use them. This last point is where traction comes in. The critical accident-avoidance skills of emergency braking, cornering, and swerving can all use up lots of traction. Each of these techniques has the potential to exceed the traction available, resulting in a loss of control.

Maintaining control while you learn and apply advanced riding skills requires effective traction management; that's your responsibility. Management of risk in a street-riding environment requires that you be aware of your surroundings and the hazards present. Likewise, managing traction requires an understanding of the factors that affect how much is available and how much you need as you ride.

What Affects Traction?

The Formula—Physics 101 for Motorcyclists
Remember that we defined traction as the friction between your motorcycle's tires and the surface of the road? If you were to crack open a basic physics textbook and look up "friction,"

you would probably see a formula that looks something like this:

$$F = C_f N$$

This expression is engineering shorthand for saying that the maximum **friction** *(F)* between any two materials is the product of two major factors. The first is what engineers call **coefficient of friction** *(Cf)* and the second is the force pressing the materials together, which is called the **normal force** *(N)*. The relationship is a general one that can be used when discussing the behavior of diverse pieces of equipment such as your clutch or brakes. To make it relevant to tires, simply substitute the words "traction" for "friction" and "tire loading" for "force." We can then say that the maximum traction for a tire is equal to the coefficient of friction times the perpendicular force pressing the tire to the pavement.

The Antidote—
Understanding the Formula

General relationships like the friction formula above are too simplistic to adequately explain everything that happens where the rubber meets the road. We use it because it is a good place to start this discussion of what the word "traction" means to us as motorcyclists. Once we have covered the basics, we can discuss practical applications of this formula along with its limitations and exceptions in the real world.

Coefficient of Friction

You can think of a coefficient of friction as a way of measuring how two surfaces interact with each other. It measures the **potential** for traction. Glass will have a small coefficient of friction against flannel. Your motorcycle tires will (hopefully) have a much larger coefficient of friction against the surface of a road. The actual value at a particular place and time is determined by the nature of the tire (design, compound, temperature, and age), the nature of the road surface (material, roughness, condition, etc.), and the degree to which the tire is being stressed (the inflation and load on the tire, whether it is rolling or

sliding, etc.). Without trying to calculate numbers the way an engineer might, we can examine some of the most important factors affecting your potential for traction on the road.

Tire compound—Generally speaking, softer rubber has a greater potential for traction. Softer rubber also wears more rapidly and flexes more under stress. A motorcycle tire manufacturer chooses compounds that balance these two concerns. Modern tire formulations and designs have significantly reduced the effects of such compromises. The traditional belief that high-mileage tires have low grip is far less true today than it once was. You can purchase motorcycle tires today that will perform amazingly well. Nonetheless, even the best-quality tires sacrifice ultimate traction for other considerations, such as long life and stability.

It is also wise to remember that rubber hardens with age and as the result of flexing. Even tires intended for sport riding will lose some of their potential for traction as they get older. You can see one of the effects of aging as small cracks form at the tire surface and on the sidewall. Inspect your tires regularly and replace them if they show significant signs of aging.

Tire temperature—Rubber is harder and less pliable when it's cold. Your tires heat up as they flex and rub against the road surface while you ride. Tires are designed to operate best at riding temperatures, so it is important to "warm up" your tires before you can expect maximum traction potential. Riding moderately for a few miles is all that's necessary to get the tires into their design temperature range.

In the recommended temperature range, your tires will give you good performance and last as long as they were designed to. Above that operating temperature range, the rubber surface will wear rapidly and lose traction potential. Keeping the tire pressure in the manufacturer's recommended range when cold and respecting the tire's load/speed ratings are the keys to preventing overheating. By following these guidelines, you will limit the amount of flexing that occurs as the tire rolls and keep the tire's temperature close to the mark.

Tire tread—One purpose of putting a tread pattern on a tire is to give better traction on wet surfaces. This is accomplished by providing channels for water to escape from the contact patch (the area of the tire touching the road). Without this path, water can't get out of the way of the advancing tire. The water literally lifts the tire from the road surface like a speed boat (a hydroplane) or a water ski skimming across the surface of a lake. When this happens to a motorcycle or automobile, it is called hydroplaning.

Tire manufacturers recommend that you replace a tire while there is still $\frac{1}{16}$ to $\frac{3}{32}$ inch of tread remaining. Tires worn beyond this point may not be safe in the rain—even though the tread pattern remains visible. Shallow grooves that aren't deep enough to channel away sufficient water may fail to prevent hydroplaning even at moderate speeds.

The tread pattern has very little to do with dry traction directly, but it can affect tire temperature, wear, stability, and even control. We've already mentioned that your motorcycle might feel "loose" when riding over rain grooves or grated surfaces. This is a result of the tread trying to follow the grooves in the road. Larger tire tread blocks (more space between the grooves) and narrower grooves generally provide greater tread life and stability, but less resistance to hydroplaning. Modern tread designs and technical advances within the tire provide excellent performance with a minimum of compromise between the goals of wet and dry stability.

Road surface—The surface material (asphalt, concrete, dirt, gravel, paint) and the presence of lubricating materials (water, ice, oil, antifreeze, leaves, sand, mud) combine to affect the potential for traction or coefficient of friction. It is difficult to generalize when so many variables are involved. Dry, coarse concrete is better than wet, smooth ice; but between these extremes you must rely on common sense and

This photograph, made through a glass plate, shows how water is squeezed from the path of a tire.

trial-and-error experience to estimate the surface's traction potential. An effective riding strategy like SIPDE is one way to anticipate and manage situations where traction may be reduced.

Normal Force

"Normal" force is the force pressing two surfaces together. (Normal in this sense is technical jargon meaning perpendicular, or at 90 degrees, to the surface.) Gravity provides this force for us as we ride, pressing the motorcycle's tires onto the road. When your motorcycle is on a level surface and moving at a constant speed or stopped, the force on the tires is proportional to the weight distribution. This distribution is typically even, about half on the front and half on the rear. Things change when you go uphill or accelerate, but we have a few other things to discuss first.

Contact patch—The contact patch, or the amount of rubber on the road, is related to the tire profile and tread design. Our general traction formula doesn't mention anything about the size of the contact patch. Does this mean that the amount of rubber on the road has no affect on the amount of traction available? This is one of those places where the formula is a little too simple to explain things. Although the size of the contact patch has no direct effect on traction, there are a number of secondary effects that may be significant under certain conditions.

If you look closely at a concrete or asphalt surface, you will see that it is quite irregular. Even highly polished, "perfectly" smooth surfaces like chrome are microscopically irregular. When you place metal against pavement, the two surfaces actually touch at only a small number of high spots. The *real* area of contact is small and independent of the apparent "contact" patch. You can think of the actual contact patch as the number of high spots. The associated friction mechanism is called adhesion.

If you put a greater area of metal against the pavement, a new set of high spots will be in contact. The *real* contact area is still small. The only way to get the two surfaces to touch "more" is to press them together. That is why normal force is in our traction equation and the size of the apparent contact patch doesn't show up at all.

Putting Them Together

The mechanism of friction between the tire and the road is a combination of adhesion, deformation, tear and viscous behavior. When two surfaces are not moving relative to each other, the coefficient of friction has one value, called the coefficient of **static** friction. The friction force decreases somewhat as soon as the surfaces begin sliding against each other. The new, smaller coefficient of friction is called the coefficient of **sliding** friction. The coefficient of sliding friction actually changes slightly with speed, but the material's behavior still follows our formula pretty closely.

Adhesion is a major contributor to the friction between rubber tires and the road surface. As long as there is no significant sliding between the rubber and the surface, adhesion is usually the dominant factor. Your tires normally roll without much sliding when you ride your motorcycle on the street. When the dominant friction

mechanism is adhesion, the size of the contact patch has little to do with your maximum available traction.

Once a tire begins to slide on the surface of the road, the situation becomes more complicated in several ways. The adhesion of rubber against pavement varies with both sliding speed and temperature. In practice, sliding friction often decreases as sliding speed increases. This effect is complicated, however, by the fact that the tire-road slip causes heating.

The sliding coefficient of friction of an elastic material is dependent on more than just adhesion. Rubber can deform under stress or tear. It also exhibits something called viscous behavior. These additional factors are interrelated, and unlike adhesion, they depend strongly on the size of the contact patch.

To make things more complicated, the contact-patch area isn't exactly proportional to the load due to tire sidewall effects. Measurements show that the coefficient of friction isn't constant; it is proportional to

$$(average\ contact\ pressure)^{2/3}.$$

In experiments, hard rubber compounds demonstrate proportionally lower coefficients of friction than soft ones on dry surfaces due to this effect.

The **tear** component of rubber friction involves the tearing of tiny particles from the rubber surface by high traction and contact stresses, causing fracture in the rubber. Very high coefficients of friction can be explained by this process. For example, racing tires typically have *three times* the coefficient of friction of truck tires.

The **viscous behavior** of rubber manifests itself in the friction process as a retardation force (or damping loss) as the rubber slides over an uneven surface. Repeated "bumps" produce vibrations in the rubber at frequencies that are related to the sliding speed and the texture of the road surface. You can hear these vibrations as the squeal of a tire sliding on pavement.

The bottom line is that the effect of more rubber on the road is complicated and not always beneficial. For example, small drops of oil may have a less detrimental effect on traction if your contact patch is larger. On the other hand, in wet weather, a large contact patch may increase your probability of hydroplaning. As an aside, fitting a larger tire does not always provide a larger footprint. Rim size has a direct influence on the size of the contact patch and must also be considered.

Big, fat tires with large contact patches are used on drag-racing motorcycles to provide high levels of traction. In a racing situation, a large contact patch permits the use of a soft, sticky tread compound. The larger contact area helps prevent the tire from overheating, tearing, and degrading to a level that would significantly lower traction.

As you can see, your potential for traction is continually changing and difficult to predict with accuracy. Remember that there are two distinct coefficients of friction: static (or "rolling") and sliding. A skidding tire usually produces less traction than a rolling one. The traction produced by skidding tires also provides no directional control, unlike rolling tires. Maintaining properly inflated tires in good condition and using proper visual habits to detect surface problems early are your principal means of avoiding skids and staying on top of traction management.

Adding It All Up

We've talked about normal force briefly, the second principal factor in the amount of traction available. Tire loading is what produces the normal force and determines how much of the potential traction discussed above is actually achieved. It's also the thing that you have the most control over from one moment to the next, because it is affected by your speed, turning radius, throttle control, shifting, and braking techniques.

Tire loading is the term engineers use for the total force that the tires exert on the road surface.

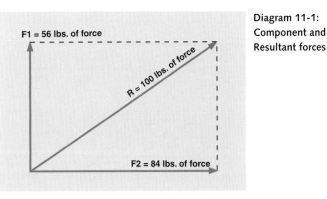

Diagram 11-1:
Component and
Resultant forces

F1 = 56 lbs. of force

R = 100 lbs. of force

F2 = 84 lbs. of force

The normal force is the component of total tire loading that acts to push the contact patch into the surface. Notice the word "component." For us to make much more headway in this discussion, it is important to understand the concepts of "component" and "resultant" forces.

Diagram 11-1 helps to illustrate the concept of component forces. The arrows in this diagram represent forces acting on or through a point on some physical object. The length of the arrows is proportional to the magnitude or amount of the forces. Their orientation represents the direction in which the forces are acting.

Forces **F1** and **F2** are two components of the single resultant force, **R.** The resultant force alone would affect the object exactly as if the two components were acting simultaneously. If you were to think of the arrows as ropes, pulling on arrow "R" with 100 pounds (45 kilograms) of force would have the same effect as if you were pulling on arrow "F1" with about 56 pounds (25 kilograms) of force, and your friend were pulling on arrow "F2" with about 84 pounds (38 kilograms) of force at the same time. Someone holding onto the ropes at the other end (where they all meet) would not be able to tell the difference without looking.

At times it is easier to see what's going on by thinking of the components; at other times it is simpler to think of the single resultant force. The important idea here is that any set of forces acting through a single point can be represented by

Diagram 11-2:
Turning on a level
surface

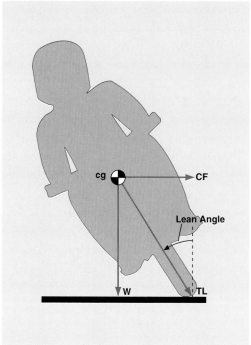

a single resultant force, and any single force can be broken down into a set of component forces that are equivalent in overall effect. Actually, many alternative sets of component forces can have the same resultant force. Similar to the way that 1+3, 2+2, and 1+1+1+1 all equal 4, you can represent a resultant force in many different ways. With this idea in mind, we can now get back to the subject of tire loading.

Tire loading can be thought of as a resultant force produced by several components. Two major components are weight and centrifugal force. To understand how tire loading relates to traction, we can break the resultant force "tire loading" down into two different components. One of these is perpendicular (or normal) to the road surface, and the other is parallel to (or along) the road surface.

These component forces act on the motorcycle's center of gravity—the place where the bike would be balanced if it were suspended from a rope. The center of gravity can be moved around by any shift or change in weight. With a rider, for example, the center of gravity will be higher than the motorcycle by itself. Once we know where the center of gravity is, we can add up the component forces and figure out how much traction we have. Remember, only the component of tire loading that acts perpendicular to the road surface makes more traction available. The component of total tire loading parallel to the road *uses* traction. Diagram 11-2 illustrates this relationship when your motorcycle is turning on a level surface.

The weight *(W)* acts vertically downward, as it always does. We can pretend that centrifugal force *(CF)* acts horizontally to your right and keeps the motorcycle from falling over as it turns. Both forces act through the center of gravity (cg). The resultant of these two components, tire loading *(TL),* also acts through the cg. The angle of the resultant force *TL* is your lean angle. In this situation, only the weight acts perpendicular to the surface, supplying the load that produces traction. The weight doesn't change simply because the bike is leaning, so your total traction remains the same as it would be if you were going straight and had no lean angle. Many riders believe that there is less traction when the bike is leaned over, so this may be a surprise to them.

The Need for Speed

When a bike is at rest on a level surface, the tire loading is simply the weight of the bike, rider(s), and cargo. The proportion of the total weight supported by each tire is determined by the center of gravity relative to the contact patches. Think of this as the basic tire-loading distribution, say 50:50 or 48:52, front to rear.

Accelerations that produce only an increase in speed cause the distribution of tire loading to shift toward the rear. The load on the rear tire increases, while the load on the front tire decreases. The effect is approximately proportional to the magnitude of acceleration; the harder you accelerate, the greater the transfer. The extreme case is known as a "wheelie." In this case, the total tire loading doesn't change, just the distribution. If there is no wheel spin due to excess power, *total* traction remains the same because the total weight doesn't change.

Similarly, accelerations that produce a decrease in speed (known as "decelerations" in non-technical conversation) cause the distribution of tire loading to shift toward the front. The harder you decelerate, the greater the transfer. The extreme case is known as a "brakie," "stoppie," or "nose stand." Total tire loading doesn't change, and as long as there is no skidding due to overbraking, total traction is still unchanged.

Vertical accelerations due to dips and bumps in the road result in momentary changes (both increases and decreases) in the tire loading and traction. One job of the motorcycle's suspension is to help minimize these effects by absorbing part of the energy and by damping any bouncing tendencies. These effects are more severe in turns because suspensions are typically designed to absorb such disturbances along the plane of the wheels and frame.

When you are moving at a constant speed, you have to provide enough power to overcome aerodynamic drag. These forces act together to shift the distribution of tire loading from the front to the rear but will not affect the total tire loading or have a large effect on traction. Depending on the frontal profile of your motorcycle, aerodynamic forces can also produce a lift or downforce. These vertical aerodynamic effects increase as the square of the speed: at 60 MPH (96KPH) they're four times what they are at 30 MPH (48 KPH). At higher speeds, they can change the total tire loading and have a significant impact on traction.

Finally, the brakes and the power train produce torque-reaction forces. These forces produce accelerations of the suspension components that cause momentary changes in the loading of the affected tire. Perhaps the best known and most obvious of these is the so-called "shaft-drive effect" in which the rear suspension extends or retracts as engine power is added or removed. The brakes can produce similar effects, depending on their design and how they are mounted relative to the suspension components. These effects are generally rather small and very brief, but they can make the difference between a rolling tire and a skidding tire near the limits of traction. Smooth throttle and brake techniques virtually eliminate them as significant factors.

Up the Hill and Down the Hill

Now we are ready to tackle the question: What happens if the surface slopes or inclines? The answer is a bit more involved because each case is different, depending on the orientation of the surface to the direction of travel.

Let's begin by looking at a turn on a "banked," "on-camber," or positive cross-slope surface. We'll assume that we have the same bike making the same turn (speed and radius) as before. The weight is the same, and since the speed and radius are the same, the centrifugal

Diagram 11-3:
Turning on a
surface with a
positive slope

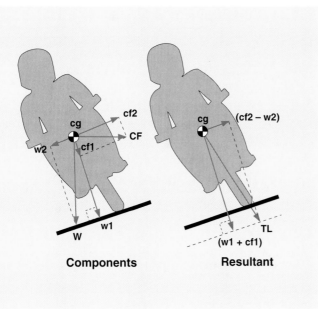

Components   **Resultant**

force is the same. We have to conclude that there is no change in the total tire loading, but what about the traction?

In Diagram 11-3, each of the two major components—weight *(W)* and centrifugal force *(CF)*—is further broken down into components that act perpendicular to the surface *(w1* and *cf1)* and parallel to the surface *(w2* and *cf2)*. These "subcomponents" must be added (or subtracted if they act in opposite directions) to come up with the perpendicular and parallel components of tire loading. This is shown on the right side of the diagram, where the resultant tire loading *(TL)* is shown with the net perpendicular component *(w1 + cf1)* and the net parallel component *(cf2 − w2)*.

On any non-level surface, the perpendicular component of tire loading due to weight alone is reduced. This includes going directly up, down, and across hills. The steeper the slope, the greater the loss of total traction due to the weight. But in a turn with positive cross slope, there is a component of centrifugal force that

makes up for this loss in traction by adding a greater perpendicular component of its own. Also, notice that the parallel components *(cf2 & w2)* act in opposing directions so the demand for traction is reduced. Greater tire loading and less of a demand for traction can combine to make banked turns excellent traction situations.

On a surface with a negative cross slope or "off-camber" turn, as shown in Diagram 11-4, the situation is not so good. The weight is still producing less traction, but now centrifugal force reduces our traction even more. Its perpendicular component *(cf1)* acts in the opposite direction (away from the surface) so the net traction-producing component *(w1 − cf1)* is much smaller than in the previous case. The parallel components *(cf2 & w2)* now *both* act downhill. In other words, traction is relatively low due to reduced tire loading, but the demand for traction is even higher.

We can make a similar analysis for each specific case, but these two examples demonstrate the principles and the ideas. The impact of these types of surfaces on traction illustrates the importance of looking well ahead and being alert to changes in the road's cross slope, camber, and surface condition when selecting a line and speed through any corner.

Most of these effects are things that experienced riders are already aware of. By understanding what traction is and how it can be affected, you are in a better position to accurately predict and manage it. Your task is to keep the potential for traction and the net force acting to press the contact patch of each tire into the road surface as high as practical when the demand for traction is high, or to keep the demand for traction at a minimum when traction is likely to be low.

The next task is to try to understand how traction is used when you ride a motorcycle. As you will see in the next chapter, it's as easy as pie.

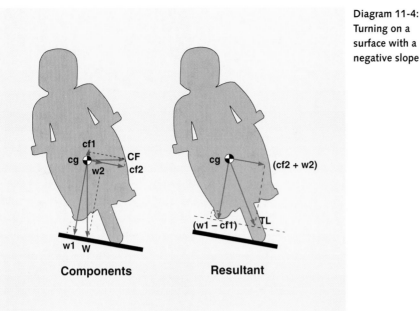

Diagram 11-4:
Turning on a
surface with a
negative slope

Components   **Resultant**

Self-Test for Chapter 11: Traction

Answer "true" or "false" to eacn statement.

1. Tires provide optimum traction regardless of their temperature. True or false?

2. One purpose of the tire tread pattern is to provide a channel for water to escape from where the tire contacts the road. True or false?

3. Under ideal conditions, the size of your tire's contact patch has little influence on the maximum available traction. True or false?

4. The potential for traction never changes. True or false?

(Answers appear on page 176.)

Maintaining Control

Once you have a fairly good idea how much traction is available, the next step is to figure out how much traction you need. Knowing where and how your motorcycle demands traction is an important part of riding with control. You already know that your potential for traction changes continuously as you ride, as does its distribution on each tire. Every riding maneuver or technique will produce a specific "traction profile," or set of forces that use up some of that potential.

One way to visualize this is by comparing the traction potential at each tire to a couple of pies. We can divide each pie into slices of varying size to match the appetite of several potential consumers or component forces. It doesn't matter whether you think of them as real pies or simply a pair of "pie charts." As you ride, the forces that use traction can share each pie in an almost infinite number of ways—as long as no one "user" demands more traction than is available. Exceeding the available traction will result in a skid, which may have disastrous consequences, depending on the situation. In other words, once the pie is gone—it's *all* gone.

Baking with Traction

The traction-pie analogy is easy to use because a pie chart graphically describes what's going on where the tires meet the road. We already mentioned that there are two pies to consider, one for each tire. The size (or area) of each pie represents the maximum amount of traction available for that wheel. By comparing the size of the two pies, you can see how the total potential for traction is distributed between the tires under varying conditions. Finally, the different-sized slices (or wedges) depict how the various consumers of traction are using that potential.

The size of the wedges is only roughly proportional to the actual forces because they don't add directly. We are concerned about traction at the road surface, but the component forces that share that traction occur in all directions in that plane; backward, forward, and to the sides. Trying to accelerate while the rear brake is applied may cause excessive wear of some of the motorcycle's internal parts, but it doesn't use very much traction! For technical accuracy, we would have to scale the wedges so they add as components (as described in the previous chapter).

Fortunately, we can use this concept to understand traction management without actually resorting to complex calculations by simply estimating the sizes of three familiar traction users. The three consumers of traction we will concern ourselves with are side force, driving force, and braking force.

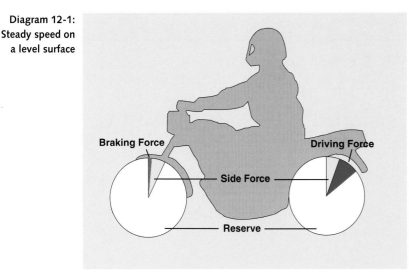

Diagram 12-1:
Steady speed on
a level surface

Braking Force

Driving Force

Side Force

Reserve

1. **Side force** includes the steering forces required for tracking, balancing, and controlling your motorcycle's lean angle. The forces required to corner and overcome gravity on cross-sloping surfaces and crosswinds are also side forces. All of these forces act primarily to the side (or perpendicular to the direction of forward motion).

2. **Driving force** is produced when you apply the engine's power to the rear wheel. You can use it to accelerate or just to maintain speed.

3. **Braking force** is produced when you apply the brakes, but it is also produced on the rear wheel when you "roll off" or close the throttle. This engine-induced braking force is simply called "engine braking." Rolling friction also contributes to braking force, acting like a small brake dragging on each wheel.

Each of these consumers has a variable appetite depending on the maneuver being attempted and the nature of the road surface. Each can consume practically no traction at one instant and all that's available a moment later. These factors are important to understand because they are the ones you can directly control—by choosing where and how to ride.

That's about all there is to it. The traction-pie analogy is simple, but it can be an effective way to look at how traction is used in a variety of riding situations. The next step is to try applying the traction-pie to some familiar riding techniques.

Slicing the Traction Pie

Let's start by considering the simple case of riding in a straight line at a slow, steady speed on a smooth, level, uniform surface.

If your motorcycle is designed and loaded in such a way that the total weight is evenly distributed between the two wheels, it will have a 50:50 weight distribution. If the tires are the same, each tire will have the same amount of traction and the two pies are equally sized.

The next thing to consider is how the pies are divided or how big a piece goes to which consumer. **Braking force** (due to rolling friction) gets a small slice from both pies, but the rear-tire portion is eliminated by power from the engine. To keep your speed constant, you dial in a little throttle and cut a slice out of the rear pie for **driving force.** This driving force is required to overcome both friction and wind resistance. Even though you are traveling in a straight line, you unconsciously make small steering corrections to maintain balance and tracking. In other words, a small slice for **side force** must be carved from each pie as shown in Diagram 12-1.

The large piece of each pie that remains unallocated is labeled **reserve.** Under normal conditions, you have quite a store of excess traction that can be called upon should you want or need to make a change in speed and/or direction. Extra traction, or reserve, provides you with a lot of control options . . . in this case.

Now let's consider what happens when you use some of your traction reserve by adding power to accelerate to a higher road speed. Since you are adding power, you must allocate a bigger slice from the rear pie to driving force. As you go faster, friction and aerodynamic drag increase and even more power is needed to maintain the new speed or to continue accelerating. The size of the slice that driving force takes from the rear pie is determined by your speed and how much the wind is helping or hurting.

All Pies Are Not Created Equal

Before leaving this case, we need to consider what is happening to the relative sizes of the two pies. When you were traveling at a constant speed, we assumed that the motorcycle's weight was equally divided between the front and rear wheels.

When you apply power and accelerate, inertial forces act through the center of gravity (cg) to increase the loading on the rear tire and decrease the loading on the front tire. In other words, more of the motorcycle's weight is transferred to the rear. When you change your speed gradually, the effect is slight. Hard acceleration can cause a significant shift of weight.

Wind resistance, or aerodynamic drag, is another thing that affects the relative size of the pies as speed is increased. This force increases with the speed of the machine, but it is also affected by the amount of headwind. Wind resistance typically reduces front-wheel loading and increases loading on the rear wheel, just like acceleration. The effect of aerodynamic drag is progressive; the faster you go, the more weight transfer takes place. Diagram 12-2 illustrates this condition.

With all of these shifts in the relative distribution of traction for each wheel, the total amount of traction is virtually unchanged. The combined area of the two pies is the same as when the machine was at rest as long as the aerodynamic forces are restricted to drag. Aerodynamic lift or downforce would modify this situation by changing the overall tire loading and result in a change in total traction and its distribution.

When you roll off the throttle, the same factors operate in the opposite direction. Engine braking uses traction from the rear tire only, just like acceleration. Most of the time, however, you use both brakes to slow the motorcycle. Both wheels can and should produce the braking forces needed to decrease your speed. The allo-

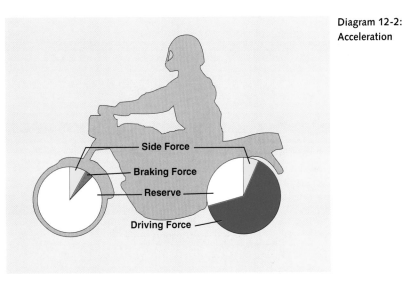

Diagram 12-2: Acceleration

cation of these forces becomes more complex depending on how hard you apply which brake and when.

Diagram 12-3 shows just one of many possible combinations of simultaneous front and rear wheel braking. Notice the relative distribution of traction between the front and the rear, and the allocation of that traction for each wheel.

Hard braking causes the front pie to grow considerably larger at the expense of the rear. The more you use your brakes, the more load (and therefore traction) you transfer to the front

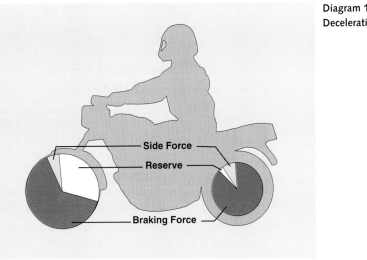

Diagram 12-3: Deceleration

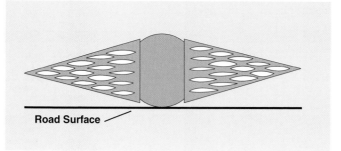

Diagram 12-4:
Tire as ice cream cones

Road Surface

tire. This illustrates why the front brake becomes more important when rapid deceleration is required and why the rear wheel is often easy to lock during quick stops.

'Round And Around And Around

Next let's look at what happens while you are turning. When you enter a constant-speed turn on a smooth, level surface, the pie slices that represent side force increase dramatically. We could calculate how much side force is used to maintain a turn by using another formula:

$$CF = mV^2/R$$

This expression says that the cornering force *(CF)* is equal to the mass of the motorcycle and rider *(m)* times the square of the velocity *(V)* divided by the radius of the turn *(R)*. This component of cornering force adds to the other users' component forces to use up more of the available traction.

The mass of your motorcycle remains fairly constant as you ride, but you can affect this part of the equation by loading equipment or carrying a passenger. You have much more dynamic control of the remainder of the equation. In other words, as you ride through tighter turns, more cornering force is involved and you require more traction. Speed is even more significant, since the cornering force grows as the square of the velocity. This means that it takes four times as much traction to ride through the same radius curve at 30 MPH as it does at 15 MPH. Side forces would use up *nine times* the traction at 45 MPH!

Sharper turns and/or greater speeds generally require more lean. One of the forces that actually causes a motorcycle to turn is called camber thrust. Camber thrust is a side force due to tire lean. A cross-section of your tires would show that they are rounded with the outside edges actually having a smaller radius than the center portion. You could liken your tires to two ice cream cones stuck together, as in Diagram 12-4. If you try to roll an ice-cream cone in a straight line, you won't have much luck. That is because the cone shape is thin at one end. Each rotation of the thin end will travel less distance than a rotation at the thick end. Since the thin end is traveling slower, the cone turns. The sides of your leaning motorcycle's tires travel along the road slower than the center in the same way. This camber-generated force combines with your steering angle to make your motorcycle turn when you are in a lean. The motorcycle must also lean to maintain balance. If you tried to steer a motorcycle around a turn vertically the way you steer a car, it would fall to the outside of the turn. You actually use this to your advantage when you ride, but that is the subject of our next chapter.

Motorcycle lean angle provides a rough measure of the cornering force because it is related to both speed and radius. This is the same thing as saying that the greater the lean angle, the greater the share of each pie that must be allocated to side force. The traction required for cornering—side force—can't be used for any other purpose. This means that less of the pie is available to be shared by the other consumers.

If you turn sharply or quickly enough, you reach the point where nearly all of the available pie for one or both tires is allocated to side force. Diagram 12-5 illustrates this condition. Any attempt to lean farther would be to ask for more traction than there is. The result would be a skid on one or both tires. In fact, doing anything that would increase the demand for traction in this situation—like adding more power or braking—could result in a skid. The demand for traction must be maintained within the amount available to prevent a loss of control. On the street, this means leaving some margin for steering control as well as a "safety" reserve. You would need to create this margin by reducing the allocation to any of the various consumers over which you have control.

For example, reducing your lean angle would result in less side force at the expense of a wider turn. If widening the turn means going into the oncoming lane or off the road, then the only option left would be to smoothly reduce your speed. Decreasing power would have the immediate effect of reducing the driving force. A rear-wheel skid would be prevented initially by reducing the total demand for traction at the rear. As speed decreases, the side force and lean angle will diminish as long as the radius of the turn remains the same.

What would happen if you rolled off the throttle abruptly in the turn? The driving force would disappear and be replaced by braking force (engine braking) at the rear wheel. At the same time, more weight would be transferred to the front tire, lessening the already limited traction at the rear. The combination of these two things could produce the skid that you were trying to avoid! Smooth operation of the motorcycle's controls prevents sudden weight shifts and greatly increases your control.

Balancing the demand for traction between three simultaneous consumers in a turn is especially difficult when each can develop a hearty appetite! One strategy for managing this situation is to try to separate the demands for traction

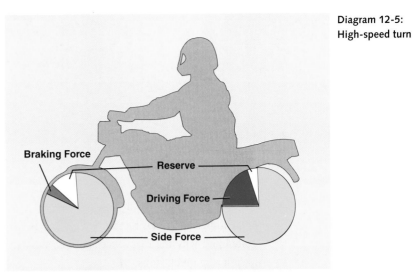

Diagram 12-5: High-speed turn

Braking Force

Reserve

Driving Force

Side Force

in time and space so that only one or two of the users are interacting strongly at any given time. You can see how this relates to the technique of adjusting entry speed while riding in a straight line to permit a gradual roll on of the throttle throughout a turn. You can also see the importance of separating traction demands when stopping quickly in a curve. The best way to accomplish that is to straighten the motorcycle ("square" the handlebars—that is, perpendicular to the frame), then apply both brakes and come to a smooth, rapid stop.

Having Your Pie . . . and Eating It, Too
To understand riding over slippery surfaces, recognize that your total traction is quite limited. This situation can be depicted by using very small pies to represent each wheel. The amount of force that consumes a small percentage of a large pie will consume a large percentage of a small pie. The limited reserve makes it easy to understand the need to keep cornering and braking or accelerating forces to a minimum. Most of the rear pie is consumed by the driving force necessary to maintain speed and the side force necessary to maintain balance and to control direction. The front pie is occupied with braking force due to friction and similar corrective side forces to the rear. There will be very little trac-

tion reserve left for changing either speed or direction in this situation.

With extremely slippery conditions, the driving force needed to maintain speed or any amount of engine-braking force could exceed the traction available at the rear. Sections of ice or areas of moss/algae covering the pavement of shallow stream fords (affectionately known as "green slime") are just a couple of examples. The precise throttle control required to eliminate driving or engine braking completely is very difficult. One reliable technique in such situations is to disconnect the engine from the problem by squeezing the clutch and coasting through the area. Your approach speed must be high enough to permit coasting without the need for significant steering input to maintain tracking and balance. If the motorcycle were to slow too much and begin to tip, the required corrective side forces could also exceed your available traction.

To this point we have been dealing with quite a few assumptions about the surface to allow simplification of the discussion. For example, we have been assuming a smooth, level surface. Once you leave this idealized parking lot for the real world, things can get very complicated in a hurry. The advantage of the traction-pie analogy is that it can work well regardless of the situation you try to analyze. The basic ideas still apply, but there are many more factors that must be considered when reality steps in.

To use the traction pie in complex situations, like a sloping road surface or hill, the relationships between the traction users become important. We discussed this type of "component vector analysis" briefly in the previous chapter on traction. You would have to analyze the interaction between centrifugal force and gravity to figure out how much of the motorcycle's weight and momentum are contributing to traction. The factors that affect your coefficient of friction must also be considered. Only the perpendicular components of tire loading (the part that presses your tires directly on to the road surface) work with the coefficient of friction to determine the size of the pies. The other components of tire loading operate along (or parallel to) the surface and are reflected in the pie slices that represent side force, driving force, or braking force.

On bumpy roads or non-uniform road surfaces, the relative size and the total area of the pies is continually changing. In an instant, one tire can lose virtually all of its traction while the other tire's pie remains relatively unchanged. Hitting a small patch of sand is one common example of this situation. If the surface is bumpy, vertical accelerations will cause the tire loading to alternately increase or decrease as the motorcycle bounces down the road. Your suspension attempts to smooth these changes out by damping, and by partially isolating a large part of the motorcycle's weight from these vertical accelerations. Despite this valiant effort, the tire loading is still affected. When tire loading goes down, the pies get smaller. This type of sudden reduction in traction is a primary reason for unexpected skids on bumpy surfaces.

Traction is obviously something we want to be aware of as we ride. The traction-pie analogy is one way to visualize and understand how traction can be managed in a variety of riding situations. Managing traction permits you to maintain a reserve for reacting to the unexpected and can be the difference between pleasant and unpleasant surprises! Effective traction management is an important part of learning to ride with control.

Smooth operation of the motorcycle's controls and practiced riding techniques can provide the tools you need to manage traction effectively. Cornering is probably the most involved of these techniques, and also the most rewarding to learn. To begin our understanding of the technique of cornering, we will start with a not-so-simple question:

What makes a motorcycle turn?

Self-Test for Chapter 12:
The Traction-Pie Analogy

Choose the best answer to each question.

1. Which of the following is not a consumer of traction?

   a. Side force.
   b. Engine force.
   c. Driving force.
   d. Braking force.

2. There is always a large amount of traction reserve. True or False?

3. How much more traction does it require to ride through the same corner at 30 MPH than at 15?

   a. Two times as much traction.
   b. Three times as much traction.
   c. Four times as much traction.
   d. Five times as much traction.

4. The traction-pie analogy only works well for analyzing ideal riding situations. True or false?

(Answers appear on page 176.)

Countersteering

13

Press Here

Countersteering is the term we use to identify the principal technique for maintaining balance and for controlling motorcycle lean angle. Despite the fact that a lot has been written about this characteristic of motorcycles, it still seems to be the source of much confusion and misinformation. We wouldn't try to teach countersteering in mathematical terms because a true, accurate, mathematical description of motorcycle-handling dynamics can be a rather imposing affair. Even expert engineers disagree over how to best model the many factors that affect a motorcycle's handling. Fortunately, the major forces that make countersteering work provide an accurate enough picture for our purposes.

Let's get back to the main question, "What makes a motorcycle turn?" We can start by eliminating a few things. We know, for example, that accelerating or braking won't normally cause a motorcycle to veer off in another direction if it is vertical and traveling in a straight line. The clutch has nothing to do with initiating a turn either. After removing the obvious, we are left with just two rider-control inputs, weight shifts and steering. If you are traveling in a straight line at 60 MPH (96 KPH) and lean your body to one side or another without turning the handlebars, the motorcycle will begin to slowly lean in that direction. You are only a small fraction of the moving mass, and the maximum distance that you can displace the center of gravity by shifting around is quite small. If weight shifts were the

primary input to turning at high speed, cornering on a motorcycle would be difficult indeed!

A motorcycle must lean to turn when it is moving even at slow speeds. The real task involved in getting a motorcycle to turn is to get it to lean. *The turning happens as a result of the lean angle.* Try to imagine riding at 40 MPH (64KPH) in a straight line on a huge parking lot. Now turn the handlebars slightly to the left. The motorcycle's front-tire contact patch will immediately start steering to the left, but what about everything else? The motorcycle wants to continue in a straight line; it has momentum. Steering the tire to the left will try to roll the entire motorcycle about the center of gravity, which results in a lean to the right. This lean creates side thrust and, aided by steering trail (see sidebar), immediately turns the front wheel to the right to make a right turn. The *turning* forces are created by the motorcycle's *lean* without any significant additional rider input. It's that simple!

If we stubbornly held the handlebars to the left, the motorcycle would lean farther and farther until we steered the tire right out from underneath us. In fact, a typical motorcycle's front-end geometry will cause the front tire to nearly "track" the curve all by itself (over about 5 MPH, 8 KPH). The turn on the handlebars feels like it directly controls the lean angle. At *very slow* speeds, the initial handlebar turn still causes the bike to lean, but without sufficient speed the motorcycle will need your help to adjust the steering angle. In this case, you would have to follow the

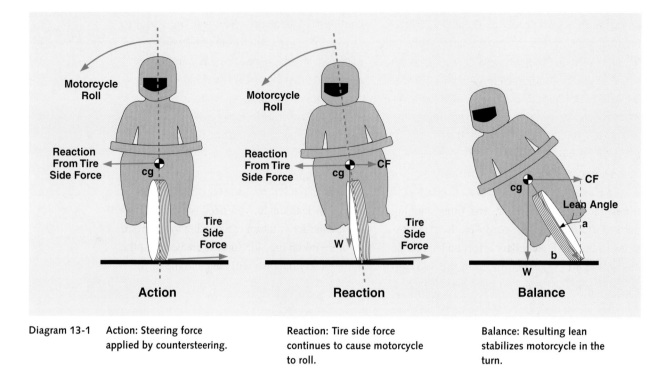

Diagram 13-1

countersteer by turning the bars in the direction of the turn.

The best control is obtained by "pressing" on the handlebar in the direction you want to turn: the direction that you are looking. Some riders with pull-back bars and a more vertical seating position prefer to think of it as "pulling" on the opposite side. Either way, you're countersteering! Pressing harder makes the motorcycle lean more quickly. Pressing longer results in a greater lean. You are using physics and the motorcycle's design characteristics to make it turn almost effortlessly!

So What's All the Fuss About?

What we have covered so far can be described with vectors, like we did for traction. When the bike is vertical and traveling in a straight line, the weight has no lever arm, and therefore no ability to counteract the centrifugal force. When you turn the handlebars to the left (counterclockwise, looking from the rider's perspective), the motorcycle's front tire momentarily steers to the left, producing a side force at the contact patch, as

shown in Diagram 13-1, "Action." This side force to the rider's left is below the center of gravity and it causes the motorcycle to lean, or "roll," to the rider's right, as shown. If the rider maintains pressure on the handgrip, the tire side force and the motorcycle's weight will work together to continue to lean the motorcycle even more, as shown in "Reaction." Looking from the tire contact patch, it appears as if a force is acting horizontally through the cg in a direction opposite the tire side force. As the motorcycle begins to lean, steering trail immediately forces the front wheel back to the rider's right to follow the turn that has been initiated. Finally, when steering pressure is relaxed, the lean angle will stabilize (perhaps after a bit of hunting) at the point where the centrifugal force and weight arrive at a standoff, as shown by "Balance."

We've covered all this before, but what we didn't mention is that this rolling effect is influenced by the gyroscopic precession of the spinning wheels. Precession is the property of a gyroscope that causes it to tilt when an attempt is made to turn its axis and vice versa. To see and feel this effect, grasp a bicycle wheel firmly by the ends of its axle and have someone spin the wheel. Then try to turn or tilt the wheel. The effect will be obvious. Since your handlebar movement turns the spinning front wheel of the motorcycle, there is a gyroscopic effect. The motorcycle leans, and that also tilts the spinning wheels in space, which causes a secondary gyroscopic effect. On most motorcycles we are also tilting an engine flywheel, and other moving parts. Fortunately for our purposes, these precessions amount to a secondary effect on lean-angle changes that is small compared to tire and centrifugal forces, especially at low speeds. In fact, countersteering "works" down to nearly zero speed when all gyroscopic forces are negligible. The major gyroscopic effects on rider countersteering occur at relatively high speeds, where a gyroscope's inherent resistance to change plays a larger part in the technique.

The gyroscopic "rigidity" of the front wheel causes you to have to press harder on the handgrips to produce the same rate of change in lean angle as the speed increases. It resists the steering input just as if there were two big springs on either side trying to hold the steering centered. As the speed increases, this gyroscopic effect keeps increasing, and you have to put correspondingly greater pressure on the handgrips to produce a deflection.

The steering effects we've discussed above operate from any lean angle. If you increase countersteering pressure, these forces will make the motorcycle lean even more. Since we are already in a lean, the motorcycle's weight has a greater lever arm (and effect). You could see the effect of the motorcycle's weight easily if it were standing still, because a lean would cause it to fall over. When you are traveling forward and release the steering pressure, the motorcycle's steering angle will tend to stabilize in the turn at a lean angle where the components of weight and centrifugal force are in balance. This also illustrates why the *duration* of the steering input typically determines the *amount* of lean and the radius of the resulting turn. To understand why the *force* of the steering input controls the *rate of change* in lean angle, you need only recognize that the harder you turn the steering to the right, the more initial tire side force is created, and the more quickly the bike will lean into the turn.

The Bottom Line

In summary, countersteering is essentially nothing more than using steering inputs to produce forces that efficiently and easily initiate a change in lean angle. It is more effective and quicker than shifting rider weight because of the greater rolling moments that small steering inputs produce. It's also easier and more precise to control than weight shifts since the smaller muscles of the arms and hands are used.

Because "push steering," as some know it, is so effective, it can seem a bit "touchy" for some riders. This is especially noticeable at low speeds where the required steering pressures can be relatively small, while the steering displacements are larger. Conscious and deliberate use of countersteering as the primary input for turning may take some getting used to, so be cautious with it until you figure it out. Once you feel comfortable with the technique, you will have made an important "discovery" that will help you ride with control.

Self-Test for Chapter 13:
Countersteering

Choose the best answer to each question.

1. What is the most effective way to make a motorcycle turn?

    a. Shift rider weight.
    b. Steering input.
    c. Shaft effect.
    d. Gyroscopic precession.

2. Increasing countersteering pressure while leaned in a turn will . . .

    a. Make the motorcycle turn in the opposite direction.
    b. Cause the motorcycle to lean farther.
    c. Bring the motorcycle back to an upright position.
    d. Steer the motorcycle out from underneath you.

3. What does the magnitude of your steering input determine?

    a. Amount of the motorcycle lean.
    b. Cornering speed.
    c. Rate of change in lean angle.
    d. Radius of the turn.

4. What does it take to countersteer at higher speeds?

    a. Less pressure on the handgrips.
    b. More pressure on the handgrips.
    c. More pressure on the handgrips and a shift in the rider's weight.
    d. None of the above.

(Answers appear on page 176.)

What Is Steering Trail?

The center of the front contact patch normally lies behind the steering axis. The distance between the point where the steering axis intersects the ground (A) and the center of the contact patch (B) is known as the "steering trail." If the bike leans, the trail produces a steering torque that tries to turn the wheel in the direction of the lean. This is a major contributor to the stability of the bike while it is in motion. Other factors include the center of mass of the steering components being ahead of the steering axis, the speed-dependent gyroscopic precession effects, and the tire properties. ■

A   B

The Camera Never Lies

It's easier to see how countersteering works in this series of photographs. ■

1. Slowing and looking.

2. Pressing on the handlebars.

3. The rolling moment resulting from the countersteer produces a lean.

4. The lean, in combination with steering trail, steers the front tire in the direction of the turn.

5. And away we go!

Motorcycle Handling and Collision Avoidance: Anatomy of a Turn . . .

Note: Following are excerpts from a technical paper presented by Hugh H. Hurt, Jr., at the Second International Congress on Automotive Safety in San Francisco, California, in July 1973.

Introduction

Most readers will remember their experiences in earlier days when learning to ride a bicycle. The experiences usually included many instances of questionable control and a few falls before the required "balance" and "coordination" were developed. Control of the bicycle seemed to demand a considerable increase in skill compared to the previous tricycle. Turning the tricycle was simple; turning the bicycle involved leaning in the direction of the turn as a result of some indistinct initial motion of the handlebars, perhaps combined with body motion. Of course, many learn to ride the bicycle in time since instinctive reactions will develop with experience. However, most riders develop these instinctive reactions without the slightest appreciation of the specific steering inputs required to enter a turn or recover from it.

The motorcycle requires the same balance and coordination for steering as well as the use of engine and brake controls. Since the typical motorcycle can operate at high energy levels, questionable control offers the penalty of serious injury to the rider. Yet the typical motorcycle rider is no better acquainted with the specific steering inputs for turning than the typical bicycle rider. All riders appreciate that the vehicle must "lean" into the turn, but the specific steering inputs to achieve this inclination are not so clear. This state of affairs is important in understanding the collision-avoidance performance of motorcycles . . .

. . . The failure of the typical motorcycle rider to brake with contemporary traffic has reasons that are distinct. These are as follows:

   a. increased neuromuscular reaction time because of dual foot and hand controls

   b. failure of the rider to use a significant part of the front brake capability because of misinformation, unfamiliarity, or fear, and

   c. degraded braking from unsuitable tires to brakes, e.g. knobbies on the pavement and dirt-bike brakes on the freeway.

These areas are surely influenced by rider experience and the problems have been exposed in time past.

It is the delayed reaction in the initial turning maneuver that does not appear to have simple or obvious reasons. The purpose of this paper is to describe the anatomy of a motorcycle turn and relate its features to the problems of collision-avoidance maneuvers . . .

. . . The main question now is, "How does the motorcycle get into this turn?"

(continued)

. . . Motorcycle Handling and Collision Avoidance: Anatomy of a Turn . . .

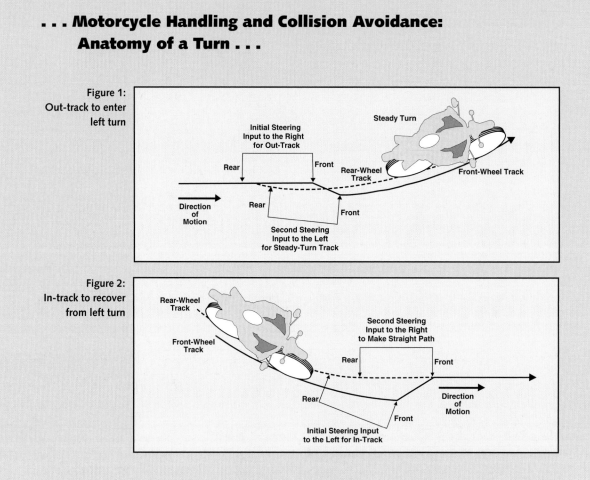

The path between straight-line motion and the equilibrium turn requires an initial steering motion *opposite* that of the steady turn. To achieve the left turn, an initial steering displacement to the right causes the front wheel to track out to the right with the rear wheel following in track. As the desired angle of lean to the left is reached, the second steering displacement is made *into* the turn to match the true track of the equilibrium turn conditions. Figure 1 illustrates the vehicle tracks under such conditions.

This process of initial out-track to turn is peculiar to the single-track vehicle and describes the fundamental steering behavior of the motor-cycle (or any bicycle). In order for the vehicle to recover to a straight path, the vehicle must in-track to reduce the lean angle and bring the vehicle upright. The recovery requires a steering input *into* the existing turn, causing the front wheel to track in with the rear wheel following in its track. As the vehicle reaches the upright condition, the second steering input is *away* from the previous turn toward the straight-ahead path. The vehicle tracks in recovery from a left turn are illustrated in Figure 2.

(continued)

. . . Motorcycle Handling and Collision Avoidance: Anatomy of a Turn

This steering behavior of the single-track vehicle has been apparent for some time. For example, Kelly[3] quoted Wilbur Wright in the following way:

". . . Wilbur used for illustration what a man thinks happens when riding a bicycle. 'I have asked dozens of bicycle riders,' said Wilbur, 'how they turn a bicycle to the left. I have never found a single person who stated all the facts correctly when first asked. They almost invariably said that, to turn to the left, they turned the handlebar to the left and as a result made a turn to the left. But on further questioning them, some would agree that they first turned the handlebar a little to the right, and then as the machine became inclined to the left, they turned the handlebar to the left and made the circle, inclining inwardly. To a scientific student it is very clear that without the preliminary movement of the handlebar to the right, a movement of the handlebar to the left would cause the bicycle to run out from under the man, who could continue headlong in his original direction. Yet I have found many people who would deny having ever noticed the preliminary movement of the handlebar to the right. I have never found a non-scientific bicycle rider who had particularly noticed it and spoke of it from his own conscious observation and initiative . . .' "

. . . The most important feature of the motorcycle steering behavior is that the first steering input is *away* from the intended turn direction. Now consider the conflict of habit patterns and reactions that can develop in collision-avoidance maneuvers. Remember that the normal steering behavior of an automobile is conventional; a steering displacement to the left is the initial as well as final requirement for a turn to the left. In the automobile, a hazard at the right is avoided by steering to the left. In the motorcycle, a hazard at the right is avoided by first steering to the *right*, toward the *perceived* hazard! If the rider reacts by first steering away from the hazard, the chances of success in collision avoidance may be eliminated or at least greatly reduced. It is easy to appreciate how the instinctive first steering away from the hazard could cause a collision rather than avoid it.

Recall that motorcycle riders are also automobile drivers and there is a distinct reaction pattern interference for collision-avoidance maneuvers.

Conclusion

. . . The initial steering input to begin the out-track cannot be accomplished by simply telling the rider to lean in the direction of the turn. If the rider leans in the direction of the desired turn without the correct steering input, nothing happens. However, if the rider leans in the direction of the desired turn *and simultaneously pushes on that side of the handlebars,* the correct initial steering input is achieved. This sort of body movement is favorable to minimize habit pattern interference, but the push on the handlebars must be emphasized.

References

3. Kelly, F.C., *The Wright Brothers,* Ballantine, 1966, p. 183

∎

Cornering
14

The Long and Winding Road

Cornering is one of the things that makes motorcycling so enjoyable. The challenge of setting up the perfect line and properly executing cornering technique is almost like ballet in its precision and grace. Many riders search for the "perfect" road, but any twisty passage can be more enjoyable through knowledge and skill. The basic cornering technique is similar for all types of roads, motorcycles, and riders. Slow, Look, Lean, and Roll . . . that's all there is to it! Of course, every situation is different, and this simple four-step process doesn't tell the whole story. That's where the challenge comes in: knowing the how, where, and why of Slow, Look, Lean, and Roll when riding through turns.

The mental activity of riding using a management strategy such as SIPDE has already been discussed a few times. Our cornering procedure is one example of applying this basic strategy to a specific riding situation. No corner exists all by itself; it is part of a ride that extends in both directions. You have to aggressively Scan, Identify, Predict, Decide, and Execute up to the corner, through it, and beyond. Let's begin with the approach to the turn and set the scene for our cornering procedure.

What You See Is What You Get

When you first see a turn in your path of travel, you face two decisions. The road is quite a bit wider than you or your motorcycle. In order to be prepared to negotiate the curve, you have to choose a path through it (or your "line") and an appropriate speed. Both of these decisions require judgment, based on your knowledge and the facts you have about the curve ahead. There is not a lot of time to assess the situation as you ride, so take the time now to examine some of the things you will need to consider.

First, you have to decide what sort of corner it is. It might be a sharp corner or a wide "sweeper." Does it stand alone, or is it a part of a series of turns? What about the radius—does the turn get tighter or widen? Remember the effect of road camber on traction and lean angle? Surface defects or hazards will surely affect your path, like conflicting traffic or potholes. Can you see completely through the corner? If your line of sight is restricted, you might have to make assumptions about several of these things.

That's a lot to find out in a short period of time. A mistake evaluating any of these facts could mean trouble. Sight is your most effective tool for gathering information. The earlier you detect a problem, the more time you have to react. It is pretty clear that it helps to see as much of the corner as possible. Remember the concept of maintaining an aggressive search with a 12-second visual lead? That applies to more than just urban situations. It may not be possible to always maintain a 12-second line of sight, but the inability to scan far enough ahead should put you on alert. You must consciously work to maximize your line of sight.

There is a subtle difference between the visual activity associated with the Scan as you approach the corner and the Look that is part of the cornering procedure. As you approach a curve you should be actively assessing the situation around you. That includes scanning as much of the curve as possible to select your line and speed before you arrive at the entry. Don't think there is no "looking" until you have slowed for the turn.

As you transition from the approach to the corner, your scanning becomes more focused on the exit of the turn. This is where you want to go, so the exit is what you need to see. That's what we mean by Look. You really have no idea what sort of corner it is and what's going to happen immediately after it until you can see the exit. If you can't see all the way through the corner to its exit and beyond, then you should stay wide and limit your speed until you can. "Staying wide" means keeping as close to the outside of the turn as you practically can, considering roadway and traffic conditions. "Limiting your speed" means maintaining a speed that will provide time and space to successfully react to situations as they first appear in your field of view. We will discuss the topic of speed in turns in a lot more detail later.

Wherefore Art Thou, Path of Travel?

You will recall from our discussion of traction management that one goal is to maximize the amount of traction reserve while riding with control. One way to do this is to control the amount of side force required in turns. Cornering force is dependent on several variables, including speed and turn radius. At a constant speed, wider turns require less side force and less lean angle. If you choose a line through the corner that uses the available width of your lane to maximize the turning radius, or "widen" the turn, you will have a greater traction reserve and more ground clearance.

Clowns to the Left, Jokers to the Right

When planning your line through a turn, one of the most important decisions is where the "middle" is. When you maximize the radius of a turn, you will enter and exit the turn on the "outside." Somewhere near the center of the turn you approach the inside boundary. The point where you are the closest to the inside of the turn is called the "apex," and where you choose to locate the apex is very important to the efficiency and smoothness of your line.

Let's consider a simple, constant-radius turn with no obstructions to line of sight, as in Diagram 14-1. The path with the greatest practical radius begins as far toward the outside as possible. Following a smooth path takes you near the inside edge of the turn at its midpoint, then as far to the outside as practical at the exit. Your apex is at the center of the turn. As we discuss different types of turns, we can compare the apex to this simple, "ideal" case.

Apex—Increasing Radius

Increasing-radius turns (Diagram 14-2) are not particularly challenging, but they can be set up poorly and feel awkward if you choose an inappropriate apex. The greatest practical radius for this type of turn places the apex before the midpoint of the turn. We call this an **early** apex. If you were to use a center apex for this type of turn, the first portion of the turn would have to be overly sharp and you would be making poor use of the extra room available near the exit.

Apex—Decreasing Radius

The opposite end of the turn spectrum is the decreasing-radius turn, as in Diagram 14-3. This type of turn is complicated by the natural tendency to select too early an apex. An early or even a center apex for a decreasing-radius turn invariably requires an adjustment in line and/or speed to prevent running wide at the exit. The greatest practical radius is achieved if you use an apex that is beyond the center of the turn, a **late** or **delayed** apex.

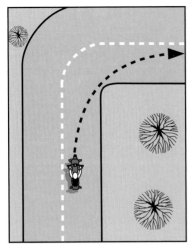

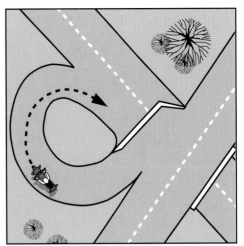

Diagram 14-1:
Simple, constant-radius turn

Diagram 14-2:
Increasing-radius turn

Diagram 14-3:
Decreasing-radius turn

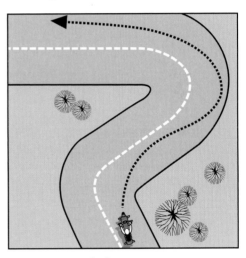

Diagram 14-4: Multiple turns

The decreasing-radius turn is the most challenging of these three types. If you are approaching a blind turn, it would be best to assume the worst: the portion of the turn that you cannot see has a decreasing radius. If you set up for a late/delayed apex, only to discover that the turn has a constant or increasing radius as the exit comes into view, this is a pleasant surprise. The late/delayed apex almost always results in greater reserves and more options for you to adjust to the unexpected. In that sense, it is potentially the safest option for any turn.

Apex—Multiple Turns

We have been discussing apex selection for a variety of single turns. There is still a fine line between each apex when one good turn leads to another, but it's not always the simplest one. The rules that we have covered for individual turns don't always give you the best line through the series of corners. Consider a sequence of two turns where the first is a constant radius and the second is a decreasing radius in the opposite direction. If you select a normal or center apex for the constant-radius section, you wind up on the wrong side of your lane to enter the decreasing-radius part. By delaying your apex for the constant-radius section, you will be in a better place to enter a path with a late/delayed apex for the decreasing-radius turn. This example illustrates why it is so important to Scan well ahead and Identify or Predict what is going to happen next before Deciding on a path and an apex for any turn.

In general, a delayed apex (as in Diagram 14-4) will maximize your line of sight until the exit or next turn becomes visible. Your choice of line after the apex permits you to maximize the effective turn radius through the exit of the turn. In many cases, the "ideal" path and apex aren't available because roadway and/or traffic conditions interfere. Once again, the use of a strategy like SIPDE is valuable in finding the best compromise.

Add Two Teaspoons Throttle . . .

Your speed changes as you slow for a corner and again as you roll on the throttle through the curve. We can describe these speed changes by focusing on three distinct points in the curve. The speed that you happen to be traveling when you first see the corner is your **approach speed.** Approach speed is determined by the environment and your ability to slow to an appropriate **entry speed,** which is the speed you are traveling when you begin the lean. We will call your speed at the exit of the turn, naturally enough, your **exit speed.** Of these three speeds, the entry speed is the most critical, because it determines how safely and smoothly the turn can be made.

Approach/Slow

The first part of the turning technique is to reduce your approach speed to a proper entry speed *prior* to the turn. This is the Slow part of the basic procedure. You already know the mechanics of this process: it involves rolling off the throttle, using both brakes, and downshifting as appropriate. The point where you should begin slowing, and the amount of braking, is determined by the amount of speed to be lost, the distance available, the braking ability of the machine under existing conditions, and your braking skill.

Selecting an appropriate entry speed can be a complex decision. Your perception of the turn radius, surface condition, and slope will come into play. You have to consider limitations on your line of sight and path of travel. These will be affected by the speed, position, and direction of other traffic and the presence of fixed hazards. Your entry speed will depend on how much of the motorcycle's available cornering performance you decide to use. Most importantly, it should allow you to respond to the worst-case scenario Predicted (the "P" in SIPDE) during the approach.

Your entry speed for a blind turn will be limited by any number of possibilities. Even if you know that the turn's radius does not decrease, something could be blocking your path of travel. Your decision is dominated by your worst-case prediction(s). Once you can see the exit, you will be able to judge all of the other factors more accurately. The information you gather works together with your experience, skill, and knowledge to define an *upper limit* on your entry speed. It is the speed that will permit a gradual roll on of the throttle from the entry point (or the point where the exit becomes visible) through to the exit. Entry speed may be lower than this, but it should never be higher.

The Slow portion of the cornering procedure ends once your entry speed is established. You are still traveling in a straight line and you have just arrived at the curve's entry point. The next step is to Look. We pointed out earlier that Look is related to the Scanning that is part of your overall riding strategy, but there is more to it.

Look

When you Look through a curve, you *turn your head* to face the exit and the intended path after the turn. Your eyes continue to move about and scan the riding environment, but the center of your field of vision is where you will be going. This is a minor turn of the head for gradual turns. You may need to exaggerate the head turn for sharp turns to face the exit. For U-turns, it means turning your head *as far as it will go.*

This technique not only allows you to Scan more effectively, it provides "visual directional control." Your mind tends to automatically make the control inputs necessary to cause the motorcycle go where you are looking. Have you ever found yourself drifting toward the side of the road while looking at some attractive scenery? That's visual directional control. Facing the turn's exit also tends to discourage looking down, which may cause balance problems. It helps you to perceive the turn as a single coordinated maneuver rather than a series of short arcs and can result in a smoother line.

When you turn your head to Look through a curve, it helps to keep your eyes level with the horizon. Some people tend to become disoriented if their head is tilted while in a turn. Keeping your eyes level helps you to better judge distances, maintain a sense of balance, and avoids possible orientation problems.

Lean

As you Look through the turn, you need to Lean the motorcycle. We know from the previous chapter that your motorcycle must lean to turn and that lean angle is most quickly, effectively, and precisely controlled through handlebar pressure. This begins a series of events, as illustrated in the previous chapter (see page 128).

A motorcycle needs to lean in a turn for two reasons. First, the lean of your tires produces much of the cornering force necessary to make the bike turn. The other reason that you have to lean in a turn is to maintain balance. When a motorcycle turns, centrifugal force acts through the center of gravity (cg) to try to lean the motorcycle toward the outside of the turn. To maintain balance, the motorcycle must be leaned into the turn so the weight can counteract the centrifugal force. We end up with a "balance" between two opposing torques, like in arm wrestling.

When you are perfectly vertical on your bike and not moving, weight has no lever arm to tip it to the side and it will be balanced when you pick up your feet. If anything moves even slightly, the weight will then have a lever arm to act, and you fall to the side unless you put your feet back down.

Let's put the bike in motion in a steady turn. Diagram 14-5 shows that the centrifugal force *(CF)* acting with lever arm *a* (the height of the cg above the ground) generates a torque to the right that tries to straighten you up. The weight *(W)* acting with lever arm *b* (the sideways displacement of the cg) generates a torque that tries to lean you more to the left. These torques are simply the product of the force *(CF or W)* multiplied by its respective lever arm *(a or b)*. When they are equal *(CF x a = W x b)*, you are balanced and

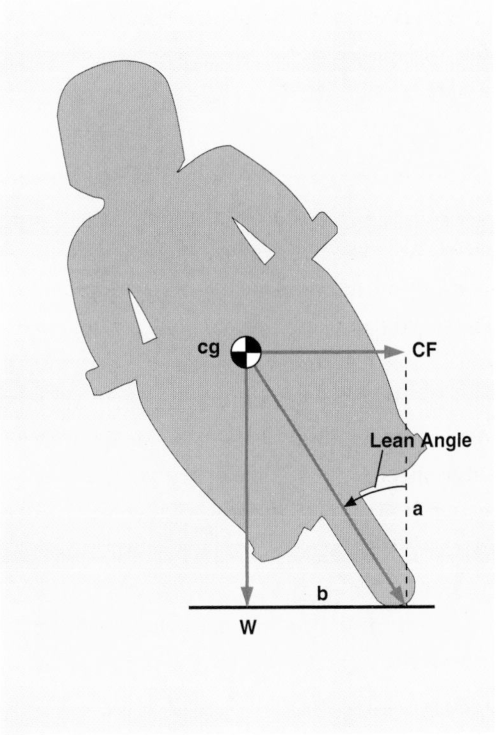

Diagram 14-5:
Basic balance
condition

the lean angle remains constant. If the two torques are not equal, then your lean angle will change until balance is restored.

When you are vertical and moving in a straight line, the weight has no lever arm to affect the lean, just like when you were stopped. Centrifugal force has its maximum lever arm at zero lean angle, and its maximum potential for affecting lean angle. Any change of direction, even slight, will involve tire side forces that create a sideways force (centrifugal force), which acts through its maximum lever arm to lean the motorcycle in the direction of the turn. *This is the principal reason why steering input is your most effective way of initiating a lean.* It is also why shifting your weight is relatively ineffective for that purpose. Since your weight is only a small fraction of the moving motorcycle, you cannot produce a sideways cg shift big enough to create a significant lever arm for the weight.

The lever arm for weight gets larger as your lean increases, and the lever arm for centrifugal force gets smaller. This means that weight has a greater effect on lean angle, while the effectiveness of centrifugal force decreases somewhat. Weight shifts can therefore be used to your advantage for making fine adjustments once you've initiated a turn. One example involves "dropping" the inside knee off the tank for a slight increase in lean angle while in a turn.

The most important idea that we can express regarding lean is that countersteering is the best way to initiate *any* turn and that shifting your body weight is a poor substitute. Countersteering is an essential part of everyday riding technique—it's not just for obstacle avoidance.

Roll

This leads us to the final step of the cornering procedure, **Roll** on the throttle. There are many benefits of a gradual roll. It stabilizes the machine on its suspension and prevents sudden changes in the distribution of traction between the two tires. Ground clearance is improved, while the centrifugal forces associated with balance are not disrupted.

We examined how accelerations that produce changes in speed result in a shift in the relative loading of the tires in the traction chapter. They also extend or compress your suspension as the motorcycle's weight is transferred. Both of these effects have an impact on your ability to smoothly negotiate a curve.

Cornering can use a significant portion of your available traction. Side forces that make the bike turn are combined with the steering and driving forces necessary to maintain speed and control. Any excess traction is your reserve for making changes or responding to surprises.

We also know that the cornering force required depends greatly on speed. For large-radius turns, both of your wheels are tracking along nearly equal arcs and traveling at approximately equal speeds. In tight turns, the front wheel tracks an arc of somewhat greater radius than the rear wheel. This means that your front tire is traveling faster and its demand for traction may be greater than the rear.

We have already discussed the factors that determine the distribution of available traction between the tires in some detail. In a curve, the traction distribution remains fairly constant as long as nothing changes abruptly. Sudden shifts in tire loading or power would result in a rapid shift in available traction from one tire to the other. This could leave one tire without enough traction to meet the demands of its users.

Traction Shifts—Abrupt Deceleration

Suppose that you abruptly roll off the throttle completely when the bike is at a large lean angle. The deceleration would cause a shift in available traction away from the rear. This might be enough to produce a skid of the rear tire if the engine braking were strong enough.

Deceleration would make more traction available at the front because of the weight transfer. This same transfer of weight will have a relative sideways component that adds to the demand for side force because the motorcycle is leaning. With more traction available *and* more being used, the balance of supply and demand may still produce a skid of the front tire if you roll off the throttle while turning.

Large lean angles aren't the only situation where abruptly closing the throttle might be a problem. The same kind of difficulties may arise at a small lean angle on an off-camber surface, for example.

Traction Shifts—Abrupt Acceleration

Rolling the throttle on abruptly or excessively may produce some more traction on the rear tire due to weight transfer, but the increased demands of driving and side force can quickly eat up any additional reserve. For very abrupt inputs, the rear tire would likely begin to slide out from under the motorcycle before any significant weight transfer could take place.

Abrupt Speed Change—Other Difficulties

Other difficulties can arise from abrupt increases or decreases of power in a turn. The suspension extends or retracts in response to changes in speed, which affects the ground clearance and steering geometry of your motorcycle. This can introduce oscillations in the suspension, which reduce its effectiveness or cause instability. Reduced ground clearance limits your lean angle and in extreme cases can result in loss of traction if parts of your motorcycle start to drag. Steering and suspension changes combine with lessened ground clearance and limited traction reserve to reduce directional stability and produce possible control problems.

Rolling Home

The solution to all of these problems is to avoid abrupt speed changes in a turn. Since greater ground clearance and extension of the front suspension tend to add to overall stability and control, deceleration can be avoided by gradually rolling on the throttle to produce a steady speed or a gentle acceleration. A gradual roll-on prevents too much acceleration or speed from driving the demand for traction beyond the limit and causing a skid.

The rewards of practiced and proper cornering technique are a greater traction reserve and a better feeling of stability and control. These are some of the goals that help make motorcycling safer and more enjoyable.

Self-Test for Chapter 14: Cornering

Choose the best answer to each question.

1. What are the two things you must choose when preparing to negotiate a corner?

   _____

   _____

2. What is the apex of a corner?

   a. Widest point of the turn.
   b. Point closest to the inside.
   c. Midpoint of the corner.
   d. Highest point of the curve.

3. A late or delayed apex is best used for what type of turn?

   a. Constant radius.
   b. Increasing radius.
   c. Decreasing radius.
   d. Off-camber turns.

4. The speed at which you enter a corner is the most critical. True or false?

5. Why is it important to turn your head to look when cornering?

   a. So that you will face the turn's exit and your intended path of travel.
   b. So you can spot potential danger in the adjoining lane.
   c. To maintain balance through the turn.
   d. To see if anyone is following you through the corner.

(Answers appear on page 176.)

Low- and High-Speed Turning

15

You Put Your Right Knee In

We have already pointed out that shifting your weight is not a very effective way to initiate a lean for turning and balance. Keeping your knees against the tank and leaning with the motorcycle in turns prevents the center of gravity from shifting and generally gives you better control and stability.

There are some cornering situations, however, where shifting your weight off-center can be used to your advantage. We will be covering some of these special riding techniques and how they apply to low-speed tight turns, turns at highway speeds, and decreasing-radius turns.

Slow, Tight Turns

Tight turns are intimidating to some riders because they require relatively large lean angles at low speeds. Leaning out or counterbalancing can make tight turns easier and more controllable. To fully understand what "leaning out" does, let's first consider why large lean angles are necessary to make tight turns.

If you were to stand next to your motorcycle, turn the handlebars full-lock to the left, and walk it without leaning, your motorcycle would follow a circle that is entirely a function of the steering angle. To ride through a turn using this same technique, you would have to go slowly and lean your body inward, keeping the centrifugal force low. It should be possible to make a circle of about the same size as when you walked the motorcycle depending on your skill and the steering

angle you can manage. Once that point is reached, the only way to decrease the turn radius further is to lean the motorcycle.

To illustrate why leaning the motorcycle causes the turn to tighten, take a look at Diagram 15-1. On the left, you see a view of a motorcycle rear tire. The front tire is not shown to keep the diagram simple. Imagine that the motorcycle is being turned sharply to the left with a nearly zero lean angle and the steering is at or near the stop, just like our previous "walking experiment." The center of the curve and the turn radius (R_0) are shown.

On the right is a similar view with a lean angle of about 30 degrees. Imagine the steering angle is still at or near the stop. The distance to the "center" of the curve is the same, but the center is now well below the surface. Neglecting wheelbase effects, you can pretend that the motorcycle is now riding around the base of an upside-down cone. The **effective** turn radius (R_{30}) is measured from the point on the surface that is directly above the center of the turn. Looking at Diagram 15-1, we see that R_{30} is significantly shorter than R_0, which means that the turning radius when leaning at a 30-degree angle is tighter. As the lean angle increases, the "cone" gets sharper, and the effective turn radius gets smaller.

Remember what happens to the relationship between weight and centrifugal force in a steady turn? To maintain balance, these two opposing forces must offset each other. With large lean angles, the weight has a greater lever arm and cen-

Diagram 15-1: The effect of lean on turn radius

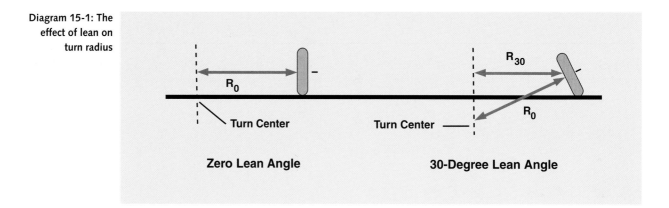

trifugal force has a smaller lever arm. This means that more centrifugal force is necessary to balance if lean angle were to increase.

Some of the required centrifugal force results from the tighter turn, but this may not be enough to balance the increased effect of the weight. If you could steer more into the turn and make it even tighter, that could produce the centrifugal force necessary for balance. If you are unable to steer more in a very tight turn, you must increase speed to maintain balance. In other words, you have to add power to turn tighter. As strange as this might seem, it is required to maintain your balance in this situation.

Perhaps you have had the experience of using a small amount of power to recover balance in a low-speed, tight turn instead of touching your foot to the ground. This works well because it takes only a small increase in speed to produce useful change in centrifugal force. You should use the throttle smoothly and gently since it is easy to get too much centrifugal force if the engine's throttle response is rapid. Using a higher gear, slipping the clutch, or using some rear-brake pressure to limit your power to the rear wheel can result in smoother overall control.

There are limits to how far you can lean the motorcycle and how much speed you can use to maintain balance. Your lean angle is limited by the ground clearance. The effect of centrifugal force (or speed) is limited by the amount of traction available and your ability to control acceleration precisely at low speed. In a low-speed,

tight turn, the front tire is tracking a much wider arc than the rear. This means that the front is going faster and will likely run out of traction first if too much speed is used.

Leaning Out

Once you are at the maximum steering angle and your speed is near the limits of traction, it would seem that you couldn't tighten up a turn any further. Leaning farther would require more speed to balance the weight, unless there was some way to lean the motorcycle farther *without* leaning any more weight. This would require a weight shift in the opposite direction of the lean. One way to accomplish this is by rider counter-balancing, or "leaning out."

Reducing your turning radius by increasing lean angle is a simple matter of geometry. The turn radius is dependent mainly on the steering angle and the amount of lean of the motorcycle's wheels. On the other hand, the balance condition is determined by the relation between weight and centrifugal force acting through the center of gravity of the rider-motorcycle combination. We can call the "lean" of the center of gravity the "effective" lean angle. If we can move the overall center of gravity away from the center of the motorcycle, we can affect balance (and speed) without changing the turn radius. This also means that you can balance at a greater motorcycle lean angle as long as you don't increase the effective lean angle any more.

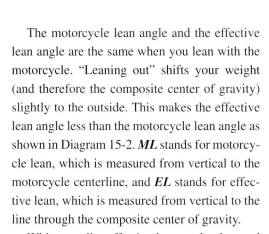

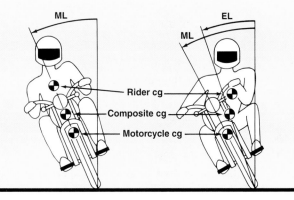

Two views of a motorcyclist leaning out to tighten up a turn.

The motorcycle lean angle and the effective lean angle are the same when you lean with the motorcycle. "Leaning out" shifts your weight (and therefore the composite center of gravity) slightly to the outside. This makes the effective lean angle less than the motorcycle lean angle as shown in Diagram 15-2. *ML* stands for motorcycle lean, which is measured from vertical to the motorcycle centerline, and *EL* stands for effective lean, which is measured from vertical to the line through the composite center of gravity.

With a smaller effective lean angle, the need for centrifugal force to maintain balance is reduced. This means that the large lean angle necessary for a small turn radius can be maintained at a lower speed than if you were to lean with the motorcycle. Your maximum lean angle is still limited by any parts that might drag. Leaning out permits cornering at a slightly lower speed in situations where traction might be lower than normal. Lower speeds also allow you to maintain a greater traction reserve. The actual amount of lean will "feel" like it is less because you are more vertical than the motorcycle.

Diagram 15-2: The effect of leaning out

ML   EL
ML

Rider cg
Composite cg
Motorcycle cg

The effectiveness of "leaning out" depends on how much you can shift the composite cg. A heavy rider on a light machine can produce a relatively large cg shift, while a light rider on a heavy machine may not be able to shift the composite cg very much at all. Other factors being equal, this means that on any given machine, heavier riders have the potential to turn more tightly at slower speeds than lighter riders. With the proper technique, every rider can benefit

Diagram 15-3: The
effect of leaning in

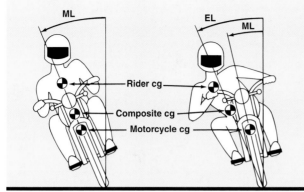

(or less) and the front-end geometry helps do the rest. Effective steering angle increases *as a result* of greater lean to "track" the reduced turn radius.

If the lean angle cannot be increased any more, the problem becomes how to increase the steering angle and reduce the radius. We would then have to prevent the resulting centrifugal force from decreasing the lean angle and increasing the turn radius. "Leaning in" is a technique that can help in this situation.

Leaning In

We already saw how, in tight turns, you can shift the composite cg away from the centerline of the motorcycle by shifting weight to the outside. This produces an effective lean angle that is less than the motorcycle's lean angle and reduces the demand for centrifugal force. If you run out of ground clearance while you still have adequate traction in higher-speed turns, the challenge becomes how to counteract *more* centrifugal force. If you can't slow down, your effective lean angle must be *greater* than the motorcycle's lean angle.

You can accomplish this by "leaning in," or concentrating more weight on the inside of the turn as shown in Diagram 15-3. Again, **ML** stands for motorcycle lean angle, which is measured from vertical to the centerline of the machine. **EL** stands for effective lean angle, which is measured from vertical to the line through the composite cg.

Leaning in can help if you unintentionally enter a turn too fast. If you enter a turn slightly overspeed and you have sufficient traction reserve, you might choose to keep the throttle on to maintain ground clearance and suspension stability; then press to lean more and shift your weight to the inside. The actual technique may be as simple as hanging out a knee on the inside of a turn, or you might shift your weight on the seat.

If you are riding much too fast, one technique is to countersteer to straighten the bike and brake

from knowing how to counterbalance in slow, tight turns.

Highway-Speed Turns

Balance is not a problem when turning at highway speeds. Plenty of centrifugal force is available for balance at high speed. The greater force requires more traction, and we have already covered traction management in previous chapters. Another concern is having enough ground clearance for the lean angles required. Centrifugal force can compress the suspension and reduce ground clearance at highway speeds. What can you do if you have to tighten your turn radius when there isn't enough ground clearance to lean more?

The simplest answer is to gradually reduce speed. Rolling off the throttle or braking abruptly may result in the stability and control problems that we discussed in the last chapter. It may also aggravate your ground-clearance problems if the suspension compresses even further. If you need to tighten your turning radius quickly when you are already leaned well over and your ground clearance is limited, deceleration is not a very attractive option. Fortunately, you have another choice, *if* you have managed your traction effectively and have enough reserve.

When we discussed slow, tight turns, we showed that turn radius is determined mainly by your lean and steering angles. You normally increase your steady-turn steering angle indirectly by countersteering. The motorcycle leans more hard in a straight line to reduce your speed, then quickly countersteer to re-enter a tighter radius at a lower speed. These methods are not recommended for routine riding. They simply give you an option if you have misjudged the appropriate entry speed for a turn. Your technique has to be precise to successfully execute this maneuver. It is especially important to look far through the curve to maintain visual directional control.

You may have seen racers hanging out a knee at the track. They use this effect to push the limits of traction and ride faster through turns. On the street, you have to maintain a reserve to deal with less predictable conditions, as we have already discussed. When you use the technique of "hanging off" to decrease the radius of a turn, you must remember that more traction is needed. Leaning in doesn't create additional traction, it simply permits you to use more of the available reserve.

As with "leaning out," the effectiveness of "leaning in" depends on the weight of the rider relative to that of the machine. Heavier riders can produce more of an overall weight shift than lighter riders, but any rider using this technique can produce more ground clearance when cornering at highway speeds.

Summary

Counterbalancing (or "leaning out") can be useful when making tight turns at low speeds, when steering angle can't be increased, or when speed must be kept low because traction is marginal. "Leaning in" permits sharper turns at any given speed when ground clearance limits motorcycle lean angle. It is useful in highway-speed turns and in decreasing-radius turns as long as there is sufficient traction.

Neither technique has any direct effect on the amount of traction available because they don't change the tire loading or the coefficient of friction. There is no magic that will allow you to corner faster than traction will allow. These leaning techniques are valuable to help deal with the limits of steering angle or ground clearance, and for the rider's comfort.

Self-Test for Chapter 15:
Low- And High-Speed Turning

Choose the best answer to each question.

1. How can you make tight turns easier and more controllable?

    a. Slip the clutch.

    b. Tap the brakes.

    c. Lean out or counterbalance.

    d. Put your foot out and use it as a pivot point.

2. Which of the following will tighten your turn radius if you can't lean more?

    a. Gradually reduce speed.

    b. Gradually increase speed.

    c. Brake hard.

    d. It's not possible.

3. When should you "lean in" while cornering?

    a. For all high-speed turns.

    b. While accelerating at the exit.

    c. For slow, tight turns.

    d. When you enter a turn slightly overspeed.

4. "Hanging off," the technique road racers use to decrease the radius of a curve, creates more traction. True or false?

(Answers appear on page 176.)

PART IV

You're on Your Way

Off-Highway Riding
16

Just because the pavement ends doesn't mean that your riding enjoyment has to as well. Many riders have turned to dual-sport riding as a way to enjoy the two worlds of street and off-highway riding.

In fact, many motorcyclists start riding in the dirt before they're even old enough to get a license to ride on the street.

Off-highway riding is an excellent and fun way to sharpen your general riding skills. You can become familiar with how a motorcycle feels when it breaks traction and slides, how it will react when surmounting an obstacle, or how to control rear-wheel skids. And if you happen to fall over (which can be one of the challenges of off-highway riding) performing such maneuvers, the consequences are generally much less severe than they would be on pavement.

When riding off the highway, you will use many of the same skills, knowledge, and strategies that have been outlined for street riding. But there's more to it than just riding off the pavement and into the dirt.

When you ride off the highway, you meet the landscape on its terms. There are no lights to control traffic, no speed limits, no painted lines to follow, no road signs warning you of what's ahead. Only you have control over what happens when you ride.

Off-highway riding involves certain risks. While the risk of colliding with other road users is much less off the highway, you must be aware of other potential risks such as rocks, ruts, holes,

and trees. The more you know, the better you'll be able to manage and reduce those risks.

Before going off road, you should know the land you are riding on and what your machine will do. Stay away from terrain that is beyond your riding abilities, like hazardous slopes or

When the pavement ends, the fun often just begins if you're riding a dual-sport motorcycle. When making the transition from pavement to dirt, it's a good idea to stop and familiarize yourself with the terrain ahead.

When climbing hills you should shift your weight forward by sliding up on the seat. You may have to stand on the footpegs if the hill is steep.

Shift your weight to the back of the motorcycle when going downhill. Use caution when applying the front brake—too much pressure can cause the front wheel to slide out or it could lock up and send you over the handlebars.

deep mud. You should be able to identify various conditions that are likely to present a hazard so that you can adjust your speed and riding style accordingly.

Responsible riders stay out of trouble not only by handling their machines well, but by being smart enough to stay out of risky situations in the first place. Often the terrain will dictate how you ride. Learn how to read it as you ride. By applying SIPDE you can prepare for potential hazards and obstacles on the trail.

Proper posture, reading the trail, and good throttle control are keys to successful off-highway riding. It's important to know how to position yourself for different riding conditions.

Keep your weight centered over the motorcycle. Look in the direction you want to go. When cornering, look through the turn and shift your weight slightly forward to help give the front tire more traction. Those are some of the basics. In addition to your physical ability to control the motorcycle, you should know what actions are appropriate for a variety of different situations.

Off-highway terrain is constantly changing—that's what makes it so fun and challenging! Rarely is the trail completely smooth or flat. The following are some typical special situations you'll likely encounter.

Hills

There are separate techniques for climbing and descending hills.

Remember that some hills may be too steep for your abilities. Some may be too steep for your motorcycle, regardless of your ability. Never ride past your limit of visibility. If you can't see what's on the other side of a hill, slow down until you have a clear view.

When approaching a hill you should:
- Keep both feet firmly on the footpegs.
- Shift into low gear and speed up *before* ascending the hill.

- On small hills, shift your body weight forward by sliding forward on the seat. For steep hills, stand on the footpegs and lean well over the front wheel in order to shift as much weight forward as possible.
- If the hill is steep and you must downshift to avoid stalling, shift quickly and smoothly. Also be sure to reduce the throttle while shifting to help prevent front-wheel lifting.
- If you don't have enough power to continue uphill but you have forward momentum and space to turn around safely, turn around before you lose speed then proceed downhill.

When descending a hill you should:
- Keep both feet firmly on the footpegs.
- Point the motorcycle directly downhill.
- Transfer your weight to the rear.
- Shift into low gear and descend with the throttle closed.
- Apply brakes to reduce speed. Be careful using the front brake. Too much on a steep hill can cause the front wheel to slide out from under you or send you over the handlebars.

Embankments and Ledges

Many of the same techniques for climbing and descending hills apply to embankments and ledges. These obstacles, however, are usually shorter in length, but steeper. *Only after becoming proficient at climbing and descending hills should you attempt these.* When riding down a ledge or drop-off, keep your weight to the extreme rear while standing, and gas it slightly as your front wheel rolls over the edge. If the ledge is extremely steep and more of a cliff, then look for another way around and down.

Climbing an embankment will require momentum, forward weighting and careful throttle control. Stand on the footpegs, keeping your chest and head forward and above the handlebars. Plan to slow the motorcycle as you crest the top of the embankment in case you have to make a quick maneuver to prepare for another obstacle.

To go down an embankment or drop-off you should stand on the footpegs and transfer your weight as far back as possible. Apply a small amount of throttle as the front wheel drops.

Momentum, extreme forward weighting, and careful throttle control are required to climb an embankment.

There are several ways to negotiate the rolling bumps, or whoop-de-doos, usually found in heavily-used sections of trail. This rider is rolling through them at a moderate pace, using his legs and arms as shock absorbers to help keep his weight centered over the motorcycle.

As your skill and confidence grow, you can attack whoop sections by accelerating while standing on the footpegs with your weight over the rear wheel. This allows the wheels to skim over the tops of the bumps and not drop into the holes between them.

Whoop-De-Doos

These are closely spaced bumps usually found in heavily-used sections of trail. They create a "roller coaster" effect when riding up one bump and then down the next one. You can approach these "whoops" in a few ways. They should be ridden while standing on the footpegs.

One method is to ride at a slow or moderate pace, keeping both wheels on the ground. Use your legs and arms as shock absorbers, while keeping body weight directly over the center of the motorcycle. Establish an appropriate speed and rhythm over the bumps.

Another method is for more advanced riders and is performed by weighting the rear suspension. Accelerating through the "whoops" while standing on the footpegs and keeping your body weight rearward allows the front wheel to skim over the bumps, smoothing out the otherwise rough ride. To avoid excessive jarring, remember to stand on the footpegs, with your knees and elbows slightly bent. It also helps to squeeze the bike with your knees to keep it from "swapping" from side to side.

Depending on how far apart the whoops are spaced, experienced riders can also turn them into a series of small jumps. To do this, accelerate up the face of the first bump enough so that you will just clear the next one. You want to land on the downside of the next bump. Upon landing, use your momentum and a little throttle to repeat the process. This technique requires a good rhythm in order to be successful. If you land a bit short and your rhythm is broken, revert back to the first method until you have full control.

Protruding Obstacles

Particularly while trail riding, you may encounter rocks, roots, logs or stumps protruding from the ground. Such objects can also deflect your front wheel if you do not see them in time.

Be sure to maintain your concentration on the trail ahead of you, scanning for obstacles protruding into your path. When riding on narrow trails, keep the balls of your feet on the footrests so your toes do not hang below the level of the motorcycle frame. This helps prevent catching your feet on such obstacles. If your bike is suddenly deflected by an obstacle, resist the temptation to stick your leg out. This may result in knee injuries. Instead, keep your feet on the pegs and shift your body position to correct your line.

When riding on narrow trails through the trees or other debris, scan ahead for branches or rocks protruding from the ground. Keep your feet on the footpegs and use your body weight to help correct your line.

Occasionally a fallen tree may completely obstruct the trail. To clear smaller logs, approach them at a steady speed and as close to a 90-degree angle as possible while standing on the footpegs. Apply a short burst of throttle to unweight the front wheel and clear the obstacle. Close the throttle before the rear wheel contacts the log.

Expect to encounter ruts in deep mud or after a heavy rain. If you find yourself in a rut, stay relaxed and allow the wheels to follow the edges of the rut. Don't try to suddenly turn out of the rut. Look ahead, not down at the front wheel in the rut.

Water and Mud

You may find more water and slippery mud in some seasons and climates than in others. In some instances, the road you are traveling may cross directly through a stream. Water and mud can conceal obstacles in your path. Damp leaves and pine needles can be especially slick. Ride more cautiously during these periods. Ride slowly and be prepared for what your wheels may encounter. Be aware also that you will have to apply the brakes much more gradually to avoid slipping and sliding of the tires on wet dirt or mud.

Your brakes may lose stopping power when wet. Dry the brakes after a deep-water crossing by applying light pressure to them while riding until they return to normal power.

While riding in water and mud, you will most likely encounter ruts.

- Maintain momentum through muddy sections. Stay relaxed, and allow the wheels of the motorcycle to follow any ruts. Don't fight the front wheel or try to turn out of the rut. Look ahead to where you want to go, not down at the rut.
- Keep your weight centered and stand on the footpegs.
- Maintain an even throttle setting. If you lose speed and the cycle begins to bog down, do not open the throttle abruptly. This will only cause the rear wheel to dig itself deeper into the mud. Instead, apply the throttle gradually to maintain forward momentum.

At water crossings:

- Beware of hidden rocks and holes.
- Learn how to read different surfaces at water crossings. The character and action of the water can lend valuable clues about the river bottom. Areas where the stream is wide and composed of shallow ripples can be good places to cross. Areas with slow-moving water or those that appear calm are often the deeper sections of the river.

Water crossings can hide rocks and holes. Maintain a relatively low speed to prevent splashing vital electrical components and keep your eyes focused on the opposite bank.

- Maintain your momentum while riding through the water, and focus on the opposite bank.
- Keep speeds relatively low to prevent water from splashing onto vital electrical components or into the airbox.
- Don't forget, fast-moving streams will tend to pull the wheels downstream. Point the motorcycle slightly upstream, if possible. Keep your weight centered to afford maximum traction so the front or rear wheel doesn't wash out from the current.

Berms

A berm is a built-up portion of dirt on the outside of a turn, sometimes called a banked turn. Heavily-used turns on tracks or trails will often have berms built up from tires pushing dirt gradually into a curved wall around the turn. You can use this wall to ride around a banked turn faster than a flat turn; centrifugal force will help keep your motorcycle in the berm. Remain seated with your weight centered, and look through the turn. But be cautious about riding near the top edge of the berm; it may give way and let your tires go over the edge.

When using a berm to negotiate a corner, remain seated, keep your weight centered, and look through the turn.

Riding through sand requires a relaxed posture and steady throttle setting to help keep the motorcycle planing the top of the sand.

It's easy for the front wheel to knife into the sand when turning.

You should shift your weight back and keep a steady throttle setting to keep the front end light.

Sand

When riding in sand, maintain a relaxed posture while keeping your feet on the footpegs and your head and eyes up, looking ahead. The motorcycle will waver in its path slightly; this is normal. Keep the throttle on and shift to a higher gear, enabling the motorcycle to gain enough speed to rise (or "plane") on top of the sand. Rolling off the throttle will effectively provide a braking action; the motorcycle begins to "plow" back into the sand as speed decreases.

When turning, it's easy for the front wheel to knife into the sand and practically stop you in your tracks. To prevent this, shift your weight to the rear as much as possible and apply the throttle to help keep the front end light.

A helpful reminder when riding in sand is *accelerate sooner* and *brake later* than you would on surfaces having greater traction. Because of the nature of sand, the motorcycle takes longer to get going and slows down much faster than on a hard surface. Therefore, you must adjust use of throttle and brakes accordingly.

If you are riding in large areas of bare sand (as in dunes), be careful of hills or dropoffs that may be camouflaged by the absence of shadows. When the sun is high in the sky, sandy hills, holes, and cliffs can appear all the same color, drastically affecting your depth perception or sense of perspective.

Rocks

Soft surfaces like dirt, sand, and grass are somewhat forgiving if you make a mistake. Rocks are not forgiving at all. If the rocks are numerous and small, the motorcycle will handle much as it does in sandy conditions. If the rocks are large, you will have to carefully select a path around or over each one. Momentum is, again, very important, especially if the rocks are loose. Smooth throttle control is critical when riding through rocks. Watch for rocks with sharp edges that could damage a tire, engine case, or low-hanging foot. Maintain a higher tire pressure in rocky conditions and make sure your motorcycle has a heavy-duty skid plate to help protect the engine.

Seasons of the Year

Ideal riding conditions are usually found in spring and fall, though many motorcyclists ride all year 'round. In summer, when temperatures are higher, be especially conscious of the effect of heat on engine and body. Be sure all motorcycle oil, coolant, and lubrication levels are sufficient. Carry drinking water along on trail rides, and protect yourself from dehydration.

In winter, when temperatures are low, be prepared in case you are stranded. You should wear warm, protective clothing and carry waterproof matches and a flashlight. If riding in snow, be careful of hidden obstacles. Do not ride on groomed snowmobile trails. Motorcycles are single-track vehicles and will spoil such trails for wide-track and flotation-tired vehicles.

Remember, *never ride alone* in any season. A buddy will be able to help you or go for assistance if needed. Plus, the riding experience is more enjoyable when shared with friends.

Navigation—Not Getting Lost

Carry a detailed U.S. Forest Service or Bureau of Land Management (BLM) off-highway area map or topographic map with you at all times. A compass will help you determine your direction of travel. If you think you may have trouble finding your way back, stack stones beside the trail in a recognizable shape known to your riding party. Use the stones to mark directions through intersections on the trail.

In wide-open areas, make mental notes on surrounding landmarks. Determine by compass your direction of travel before you leave your base camp. Take an occasional look behind you on the way out so you know what the ride will look like when you return. If someone is staying in camp while you go riding, let them know where you intend to go.

Carefully select your path when riding in rocky terrain. Keep your toes pointed up to avoid smashing your foot between the rock and footpeg.

Plan your route using a U.S. Forest Service, Bureau of Land Management (BLM) or topographic map to help prevent you and your group from getting lost.

Know the Laws

The laws and regulations that control how and where you use your off-highway motorcycle are important. They help to keep you out of trouble; they keep the sport healthy by controlling less responsible riders; they help protect the land you ride on and the people who own it. Always obey posted signs. Motorcycle dealers and off-highway motorcycle clubs can often provide you with a summary of local laws or direct you to park rangers, game wardens, or others who will be glad to help you.

You and the Rest of the World

There's one fundamental factor that controls your riding—access to land. Developing and maintaining riding opportunities means getting along with the rest of the world—private land-owners, public land managers, and people you meet on trails. The better you get along with all these people, the easier it will be to find and keep good riding areas.

Find a Place to Ride

Some sources for finding places to ride are:

- Your motorcycle dealer
- Off-highway motorcycle clubs or associations
- State maps (features and topographical)
- U.S. Forest Service
- Bureau of Land Management
- State agencies such as Parks & Recreation, Fish & Game, or Forestry.

Entering organized events like enduros, hare scrambles, and poker runs can be a great way to ride new trails. Clubs often get access for specific events to trails and areas that are closed the rest of the time.

You and Mother Nature

Riding behavior that harms the land is self-defeating and irresponsible. Learn to protect and preserve your riding areas, in other words, TREAD LIGHTLY.

- Obtain a travel map whenever possible, and check which trails are open or closed. Learn the rules and follow them.

- Keep your motorcycle quiet. Don't make your exhaust system noisier—there is nothing people dislike more than a loud off-highway vehicle. Keep your spark arrester in place.
- Avoid running over young trees, shrubs, and grasses—damaging or killing them.
- Stay off soft, wet roads and trails readily torn up by vehicles (particularly during hunting seasons). Repairing the damage is expensive.
- Travel around meadows, steep hillsides, or stream banks and lakeshores that are easily scarred by churning wheels.
- Resist the urge to pioneer a new road or trail, or to cut across a switchback.
- Use courtesy when you meet others on the trail. Pull off and give right of way to horse-back riders or hikers. It is best to shut off the engine whenever near horses—a panicked horse is a danger to you and its rider.
- Never chase animals or otherwise subject them to stress. Stress can sap their scarce energy reserves.
- Obey gate closures and regulatory signs. Vandalism costs tax dollars.
- Stay out of wilderness areas. They're closed to all vehicles. Know where the boundaries are.
- Get permission to travel across private land. Respect landowner rights.

Future opportunities for exciting travel with your off-highway motorcycle are in your hands—TREAD LIGHTLY!

Other Safe Riding Practices

Here are a few more tips to make your off-highway motorcycling experience safe and enjoyable:

- Always perform a pre-ride inspection of your motorcycle (see the T-CLOCK checklist, Appendix A).
- Ride in the company of others so that you can assist each other in the event of trouble.
- Wear bright clothing to increase visibility to others.

- Carry a first-aid pack and tool/repair kit with you.
- Carry some snacks and drinking water.
- Youngsters should not ride motorcycles that are too tall or powerful for their capabilities.
- Watch for hidden obstacles in sandy, snowy, or muddy conditions.
- Except for dual-purpose machines, off-highway motorcycles are not designed for use on pavement. They should never be ridden on the highway or any public roadways.
- Tell someone where you are going and when you plan to return.
- Avoid following too closely behind another rider and restricting your visibility.

Registration

In many states the law requires that you register your motorcycle as part of the state's off-highway vehicle-registration program. Fines for riding unregistered vehicles can get expensive, to say nothing of the risk of having your off-highway motorcycle impounded. Besides, most states use the registration fees to develop riding trails and facilities. So by registering your motorcycle, you and your friends may be helping to buy or maintain places to ride.

Four-Wheel Off-Roading

There are other forms of off-highway vehicles that motorcyclists may want to ride. One of those is the all-terrain vehicle, or ATV. ATVs handle differently from other vehicles, such as motorcycles and cars. ATVs are rider-active; to enhance the performance capabilities of the ATV, you must shift your body weight. This is especially true in maneuvers such as turning, negotiating hills, and crossing obstacles.

Whether you ride off-highway on two wheels or four, it's always a good idea to receive the proper instruction. The ATV Safety Institute has classes in both off-highway motorcycle and ATV operation. To enroll in a class near you, call (800) 887-2887.

Self-Test for Chapter 16: Off-Highway Riding

Answer "true" or "false" to each statement.

1. Off-highway riding requires a completely different set of skills, knowledge, and strategies than used in street riding. True or false?

2. Applying SIPDE is just as effective to prepare for hazards while off-highway riding as it is while riding on the street. True or false?

3. There are no laws that govern off-highway riding. True or false?

4. You should Tread Lightly to protect and preserve off-highway riding areas. True or false?

(Answers appear on page 176.)

The Road Ahead

17

We have covered many subjects while discussing motorcycling excellence. But it comes down to one major goal—to increase your enjoyment of riding.

Each of us is unique when it comes to the mental and physical environments that make up our world of motorcycling:

- Our motorcycles have individual traits.
- The roads we ride are continually changing.
- And, as individuals, we each have different ways of reacting to situations and different levels of physical skill.

Excellence in our motorcycling experience equates to an ever-increasing appreciation of all of these things. There are three steps in committing to our motorcycling future:

- awareness
- knowledge
- and riding within our limits.

Only you can take responsibility for awareness and riding within your limits. But you can gain more knowledge with the help of others. You can read books on motorcycling, as you are now; or motorcycle magazines, most of which carry great tips on being a proficient motorcyclist in every issue. Another path to knowledge is through training. This gives you goals: maneuvers to practice.

Traffic-safety experts widely acknowledge the Motorcycle Safety Foundation's *RiderCourses* as the best introduction to motorcycling anywhere in the world. If you're a beginning rider, the *Motorcycle RiderCourse: Riding and Street Skills* will put you on the road to safety, right from the start. Even if you're a veteran rider, the *Experienced RiderCourse* will fine-tune your skills. Over 1 million motorcyclists have graduated from a *RiderCourse*. Shouldn't you? Here are just four of the benefits:

- greater confidence
- greater safety
- licensing-test waivers (in over 20 states)
- insurance discounts (through many companies).

Motorcycle RiderCourse

The *Motorcycle RiderCourse: Riding and Street Skills* is aimed at beginning riders of all ages. A minimum of seven hours' classroom instruction prepares the student for at least eight hours of practical riding in a controlled, off-street environment—for example, a parking lot. Motorcycles and helmets are included in your course fee (if any). The motorcycles are smaller-displacement machines, under 350cc, and often loaned by local dealers.

You'll learn how to operate a motorcycle safely, with a lot of emphasis on the special skills and mental attitude necessary for dealing with traffic.

Your coaches are certified by the Motorcycle Safety Foundation. They'll start you off with straight-line riding, turning, shifting and stopping. You'll gradually progress to cornering, swerving, and emergency braking.

In the classroom you'll learn about the different types of motorcycles, their controls, and what to check before you ride. The instructors—all experienced motorcyclists—will advise you on what to wear for protection and comfort. You'll find out how alcohol and other drugs affect your ability to ride safely. A very important segment of the course will show you how to create your own strategy for riding in traffic, and dealing with critical situations.

The course concludes with two exams: a written knowledge test and a riding-skills test. You'll smile with satisfaction as the instructor hands you that course-completion card!

Experienced RiderCourse

Even if you've been riding for some time, there's always something left to learn. Increasing numbers of seasoned riders are flocking to the eight-hour *Experienced RiderCourse* to hone their skills and fine-tune the mental drills needed for survival in today's traffic.

In the classroom you'll discuss with your peers how to balance the mental and physical aspects of safe riding, manage risk, increase visibility and optimize your lane position. The *Experienced RiderCourse* also covers protective gear, rider responsibility, motorcycle inspection and care, the effects of alcohol and other drugs on riding, and a skill evaluation and knowledge test.

Using your own motorcycle, you'll put into practice the techniques of managing traction, controlling rear-wheel skids, stopping quickly, cornering, and swerving by countersteering.

Finding a RiderCourse

With nearly 1,000 *RiderCourse* sites throughout the United States, there's probably one near you. Courses are taught by high schools, colleges, universities, continuing-education programs, civic groups, police departments, motorcycle clubs, and state safety programs. Successful completion of a *RiderCourse* is mandatory for all motorcyclists in the armed forces.

Course fees vary from state to state and from program to program; some are free to the student, thanks to fees on motorcyclist-license endorsements and motorcycle registrations. Some motorcycle distributors and brand-sponsored clubs will reimburse all or part of your tuition. To find a course near you, call: 1-800-447-4700.

A motorcycle is an exciting vehicle. Part of the excitement is the physical skills we use to ride. It's more challenging than driving a car, but most of us wouldn't trade the experience for anything.

To enhance that experience, get your license, practice the skills you've learned every time you ride, and use your newfound knowledge wisely. It's a good foundation for safe, enjoyable motorcycling—because the more you know, the better it gets!

Your Concerns About Riding

When was the last time someone gave you a pointer or two on your riding technique? Did they tell you what you were doing wrong, or maybe tell you how to fix it?

When you ride, where do you feel the most confident? On the Interstate? On that mountain road with all the curves? What makes you feel a little uneasy? Making quick moves in heavy city traffic? Making tight maneuvers in the parking lot with your friends watching? Negotiating that country road with a few too many potholes, sand, and even gravel?

Think for a moment about your concerns about riding. Is one of them the repair cost from even a minor tip-over?

Do some these things distract from your enjoyment of riding?

We sometimes talk about the "flow"—or things "just happening"—when we ride. The more you can make advanced riding skills instinctive, the easier it is to use them when you need them. ■

T-CLOCK Inspection

T-CLOCK ITEM	WHAT TO CHECK	WHAT TO LOOK FOR	CHECK-OFF	
T — TIRES & WHEELS				
Tires	Condition	Tread depth, wear, weathering, evenly seated, bulges, imbedded objects.	Front	Rear
	Air Pressure	Check when cold, adjust to load/speed.	Front	Rear
Wheels	Spokes	Bent, broken, missing, tension, check at top of wheel "ring" OK — "thud," loose spoke.	Front	Rear
	Cast	Cracks, dents.	Front	Rear
	Rims	Out of round/true = 5mm. Spin wheel, index against stationary pointer.	Front	Rear
	Bearings	Grab top and bottom of tire and flex: No freeplay (click) between hub and axle, no growl when spinning.	Front	Rear
	Seals	Cracked, cut or torn, excessive grease on outside, reddish-brown around outside.	Front	Rear
C — CONTROLS				
Levers	Condition	Broken, bent, cracked, mounts tight, ball ends on handlebar lever.	Front	Rear
	Pivots	Lubricated.		
Cables	Condition	Fraying, kinks, lubrication: ends and length.		
	Routing	No interference or pulling at steering head, suspension, no sharp angles, wire looms in place.		
Hoses	Condition	Cuts, cracks, leaks, bulges, chafing, deterioration.		
	Routing	No interference or pulling at steering head, suspension, no sharp angles, wire looms in place.		
Throttle	Operation	Moves freely, snaps closed, no revving.		
L — LIGHTS				
Battery	Condition	Terminals, clean and tight, electrolyte level, held down securely.		
	Vent Tube	Not kinked, routed properly, not plugged.		
Lenses	Condition	Cracked, broken, securely mounted, excessive condensation.		
Reflectors	Condition	Cracked, broken, securely mounted.		
Wiring	Condition	Fraying, chafing, insulation.		
	Routing	Pinched, no interference or pulling at steering head or suspension, wire looms and ties in place, connectors tight, clean.		
Headlamp	Condition	Cracks, reflector, mounting and adjustment system.		
	Aim	Height and right/left.		

T-CLOCK ITEM	WHAT TO CHECK	WHAT TO LOOK FOR	CHECK-OFF	
O — OIL				
Levels	**Engine Oil**	Check warm on centerstand, dipstick, sight glass.		
	Hypoid Gear Oil	Transmission, rear driver, shaft.		
	Hydraulic Fluid	Brakes, clutch, reservoir or sight glass.		
	Coolant	Reservoir and/or coolant recovery tank — cool only.		
	Fuel	Tank or gauge.		
Leaks	**Engine Oil**	Gaskets, housings, seals.		
	Hypoid Gear	Gaskets, seals, breathers.		
	Hydraulic Fluid	Hoses, master cylinders, calipers.		
	Coolant	Radiator, hoses, tanks, fittings, pipes.		
	Fuel	Lines, fuel taps, carbs.		
C — CHASSIS				
Frame	**Condition**	Cracks at gussets, accessory mounts, look for paint lifting.		
	Steering-Head Bearings	No detent or tight spots through full travel, raise front wheel, check for play by pulling/pushing forks.		
	Swingarm Bushings/ Bearings	Raise rear wheel, check for play by pushing/pulling swingarm.		
Suspension	**Forks**	Smooth travel, equal air pressure/damping anti-dive settings.	Left	Right
	Shock(s)	Smooth travel, equal pre-load/air pressure/damping settings, linkage moves freely and is lubricated.	Left	Right
Chain or Belt	**Tension**	Check at tightest point.		
	Lubrication	Side plates when hot. *Note:* do not lubricate belts.		
	Sprockets	Teeth not hooked, securely mounted.		
Fasteners	**Threaded**	Tight, missing bolts, nuts.		
	Clips	Broken, missing.		
	Cotter Pins	Broken, missing.		
K — KICKSTAND				
Centerstand	**Condition**	Cracks, bent.		
	Retention	Springs in place, tension to hold position.		
Sidestand	**Condition**	Cracks, bent (safety cut-out switch or pad if equipped).		
	Retention	Springs in place, tension to hold position.		

State Motorcycle Operator Licensing Information

Legend to Licensing Table

Auto Test – Automated Testing available as of 1990.

Primary – Tests used in most or all urban locations and/or where the majority of motorcyclists are tested.

Secondary – Test used in rural sites or locations unable to accomodate the primary test.

Rider-Ed Waivers – Issued to eligible applicants who successfully complete rider-education requirements acceptable for licensing standards.

Out-of-State Transfer (Reciprocal) Waivers – Issued to eligible applicants who were tested and licensed in a previous jurisdiction and maintain acceptable standards for current jurisdiction.

K – Knowledge

Sk – Skill

Motorcycle Operator Manual and Knowledge Tests

The Motorcycle Operator Manual includes information on motorcycle riding preparations, protective gear, defensive operating. Each of the 5 Knowledge Tests that include 25 multiple-choice questions are based on MOM information. Tests emphasize areas critical to safe riding.

MSF Off-Street Tests

The Alternative Motorcycle Operator Skill Tests (Alternative MOST) requires:

- applicant performance of 5 basic vehicle-control exercises (Stalling, Sharp Turn, Normal Stop, Cone Weave, and U-Turn).
- applicant performance of 2 collisioin avoidance exercises (Quick Stop and Swerve).

The Motorcyclist Licensing Skill Test (MLST) requires:

- performance of 1 basic vehicle-control exercise (Straight Path & Sharp Turn).
- performance of 2 collision-avoidance exercises (Riding a Curve, and Quick Stop/Swerve).
- repetition of collision-avoidance exercises that allows more opportunity to assess turning, stopping and swerving skills.

MSF On-Street Test

The Motorcyclist In-Traffic Test (MIT):

- requires applicant performance of 8-11 riding behaviors determined to be important to safer riding.
- allows assessment of rider judgment in actual traffic situations.
- does not require off-street test facility.

Motorcyclist Knowledge Testing				Motorcyclist Skill Testing					
Handbook Used	Knowledge Tests	Auto Test.	State	Primary Skill Test	Secondary Skill Tests	Rider-Ed Waiver	Reciprocal Waivers	3-Wheel/Sidecar Testing	3 Wh/Sc Oper Restricted to
Local	Local	no	AL	none	none	no	Sk	none	none
MOM	MSF	yes	AK	Alt. MOST	Local off-street	no	Sk	mod m/c skill test	full m/c priv
MOM	mod. MSF	no	AZ	MLST	Alt. MOST	Sk	Sk,K	mod m/c skill test	sidecar, 3-wh
Local	Local	yes	AR	Local on-street	Local on-street	no	Sk,K	mod m/c skill test	full m/c priv
Local	Local	no	CA	Local off-street	Local off-street	Sk	Sk	car skill test	sidecar, 3-wh
mod. MOM	MSF	no	CO	Alt. MOST	Local on-street	Sk	Sk	mod m/c skill test	sidecar, 3-wh
MOM	MSF	yes	CT	Alt. MOST	none	Sk	Sk,K	car skill test	full m/c priv
MOM	MSF	no	DE	Alt. MOST	Alt. MOST	Sk,K	Sk	car skill test	full DL priv
Local	Local	no	DC	Alt. MOST	Local off-street	no	Sk	car skill test	full m/c priv
MOM	Local	yes	FL	Alt. MOST	MLST	Sk,K	Sk,K	car skill test	sidecar, 3-wh
MOM	MSF	no	GA	MLST	MLST	Sk,K	Sk	car skill test	sidecar, 3-wh
MOM	MSF	no	HI	Alt. MOST	Alt. MOST	no	Sk	mod m/c skill test	sidecar, 3-wh
mod.MOM	mod. MOM	yes	ID	New legislation—pending further development					
mod. MOM	Local	no	IL	Alt. MOST	Local on-street	Sk	Sk	mod m/c skill test	sidecar, 3-wh
MOM	MSF	no	IN	Alt. MOST	Alt. MOST	Sk	Sk	mod m/c skill test	sidecar, 3-wh
MOM	MSF	no	IA	Local off-street	Local off-street	Sk	Sk	mod m/c skill test	sidecar, 3-wh
MOM	MSF	no	KS	Alt. MOST	Alt. MOST	Sk	Sk	mod m/c skill test	full m/c priv
Local	Local	yes	KY	Local off-street	Local off-street	Sk	Sk	mod m/c skill test	full m/c priv
mod. MOM	MSF	no	LA	Local off-street	Local off-street	Sk	Sk,K	none	full m/c priv
mod. MOM	Local	no	ME	Local on-street	Local on-street	K	Sk	car skill test	
mod. MOM	MSF	yes	MD	Local off-street	Local off-street	no	Sk	car skill test	multi-purp. veh.
Local	Local	yes	MA	Local Off-street	Local off-street	no	Sk,K	mod m/c skill test	sidecar, 3-wh
MOM	MSF	no	MI	Alt. MOST	Local off-street	Sk	Sk	mod m/c skill test	sidecar, 3-wh
MOM	Local	yes	MN	Alt. MOST	Alt. MOST	no	Sk	mod m/c skill test	3-wh
MOM	Local	no	MS	M/C In-Traffic	Local on-street	no	Sk	car skill test	sidecar, 3-wh
MOM	mod. MSF	no	MO	Local off-street	Local on-street	no	Sk,K	mod m/c skill test	sidecar, 3-wh
MOM	MSF	no	MT	Alt. MOST	Local on-street	Sk	Sk	mod m/c skill test	sidecar, 3-wh
MOM	MSF	no	NE	Alt. MOST	M/C In-Traffic	Sk,K	Sk	car skill test	full m/c priv
MOM	MSF	yes	NV	MLST	MLST	Sk	Sk	car skill test	sidecar, 3-wh
Local	Local	no	NH	Alt. MOST	Alt. MOST	Sk	Sk	car skill test	full m/c priv
mod. MOM	Local	yes	NJ	Alt. MOST	Alt. MOST	no	Sk	mod m/c skill test	sidecar, 3-wh
MOM	MSF, Local	no	NM	Alt. MOST	Local on-street	Sk,K	Sk,K	mod m/c skill test	full m/c priv
MOM	Local	no	NY	Local on-street	Local on-street	no	Sk,K	mod m/c skill test	sidecar, 3-wh
MOM	Local	no	NC	Local off-street	Local off-street	no	Sk	none	full m/c priv
MOM	MSF	no	ND	Alt. MOST	Local off-street	no	Sk	mod m/c skill test	sidecar, 3-wh
MOM	Local	no	OH	Local off-street	Local off-street	no	Sk	mod m/c skill test	sidecar, 3-wh
Local	Local	no	OK	M/C In-Traffic	Local on-street	no	Sk	mod m/c skill test	full m/c priv
MOM	MSF	yes	OR	Alt. MOST	Alt. MOST	Sk	Sk	mod m/c skill test	sidecar, 3-wh
mod. MOM	Local	yes	PA	Local off-street	Local off-street	Sk,K	Sk	mod m/c skill test	sidecar, 3-wh
Local	Local	no	RI	Local off-street	Alt. MOST	Sk,K	Sk	mc RE course	full m/c priv
mod. MOM	mod. MSF	yes	SC	Local off-street	Local off-street	no	Sk	no info	sidecar, 3-wh
MOM	MSF	no	SD	M/C In-Traffic	Local on-street	Sk,K	Sk	car skill test	full m/c priv
MOM	mod. MSF	no	TN	Local on-street	Local on-street	Sk	Sk,K	car skill test	full m/c priv
Local	Local	yes	TX	Local on-street	Local on-street	no	Sk	none	full m/c priv
MOM	Local	no	UT	Alt. MOST	Local off/on	Sk	Sk,K	mod m/c skill test	sidecar, 3-wh
Local	Local	no	VT	Alt. MOST	Alt. MOST	no	Sk	none	sidecar, 3-wh
MOM	MSF	no	VA	Local on-street	Alt. MOST	Sk	Sk,K	no info	full m/c priv
mod. MOM	MSF	no	WA	Alt. MOST	Alt. MOST	no	Sk	car skill test	sidecar, 3-wh
MOM	MSF	no	WV	Alt. MOST	Alt. MOST	Sk,K	Sk,K	no info	no info
MOM	mod. MSF	no	WI	M/C In Traffic	M/C In Traffic	Sk	Sk,K	mod m/c skill test	sidecar, 3-wh
MOM	MSF	no	WY	Local off-street	Local off-street	no	Sk,K	mod m/c skill test	full m/c priv

State Motorcycle Equipment Requirements

Legend for Motorcycle Equipment Table
(Compiled by Motorcycle Industry Council — March, 1994)

• Requirement in law

* If carrying a passenger

1. Reflectorization

2. Where speeds exceed 35 mph

3. With learner's permit; for 1 yr. after obtaining license; & passengers under 15 yrs.

4. Under 18 years

5. Operators under 21 yrs.; for 1 yr. after obtaining license; & all passengers

6. Under 21 years

7. Possession by all, wear under 19 years & by instruction permit holders

8. Novice license holders

9. Prohibited except for communication

10. Left side

11. Left and right side

12. One wheel

13. Both wheels

14. Maximum of 10 inches above fasten point

15. Maximum of 12 inches above fasten point

16. Maximum of 15 inches above fasten point

17. Maximum of 15 inches above seat

18. Maximum of 30 inches above seat

19. Handgrips below shoulder height

20. Speedometer

21. For motorcylce manufactured after 1/1/78

22. Odometer

23. Annual emissions inspection

24. Upon transfer of title

25. Random

a. If originally equipped by manufacturer

b. For motorcycle manufactured after 1/1/73

c. For motorcycle manufactured after 7/1/74

d. For motorcycle manufactured after 4/1/77

e. For motorcycle manufactured after 1/1/80

f. For motorcycle manufactured after 9/1/80

g. For 1974 or later model year motorcycle

h. For 1977 or later model year motorcycle

i. Manufacturer requirement for motorcycle manufactured after 1/1/78

j. Except if equipped with windscreen

k. Except if equipped with windscreen 15 inches or higher

m. Instructional permit holders

n. Prohibited in both ears simultaneously

o. Except helmets with speakers

#Required by inspection regulations

STATE MOTORCYCLE EQUIPMENT REQUIREMENTS

As of March 1994 — State	Safety Helmet	Eye Protection	Rearview Mirror	Brakes	Handlebar Height	Passenger Seat*	Passenger Footrests*	Passenger Handhold*	Headphones Prohibited	Turn Signals	Speedometer/Odometer	Headlight Daytime Use	Periodic Inspection
Alabama	•		•	•-13	•-17	•	•						
Alaska	•-4	•-k	•-11	•-13	•-17	•	•	•	•				•-25
Arizona	•-4	•-j	•	•-12	•-17	•	•	•					•-23
Arkansas	•	•	•	•-12		•	•					•	•
California	•		•	•-13	•-19	•	•		•-n	•-b		•-i	•-25
Colorado		•	•	•-12		•	•		•-o				•-25
Connecticut	•-4	•-j	•	•-13,g	•-17	•	•					•-e	•-25
Delaware	•-1,7	•	•	•-12	•-17	•	•			•			•
District of Columbia	•	•-j	•	•-13	•-17,#	•	•	•			•-20		•
Florida	•	•	•	•-13	•-17	•	•		•-o			•	
Georgia	•	•-j	•	•-12	•-17	•	•		•-9			•	
Hawaii	•-1,4	•-j	•	•-12	•-17	•	•						•
Idaho	•-4		•	•-12		•	•						
Illinois		•	•	•-12	•-19	•	•		•-o			•	
Indiana	•-4,m	•-4	•	•-13	•-17	•	•					•	
Iowa			•	•-12	•-17	•	•				•	•-h	
Kansas	•-4	•-j	•	•	•-19	•	•			•-b		•-21	•-25
Kentucky	•	•	•	•-12		•	•						
Louisiana	•	•-j	•-10	•-12	•-17	•	•						•
Maine	•-3		•	•-12	•-19	•	•					•	•
Maryland	•-1	•-j	•-11	•-12	•-17	•	•	•-#	•-n		•-#		•-24
Massachusetts	•	•-j	•	•-13	•-17	•	•		•				•
Michigan	•	•-2,j	•	•-13	•-17	•							•-25
Minnesota	•-4,m	•-j	•	•-12	•-19	•	•		•-n			•	•-25
Mississippi	•		•	•-12	•-14,#						•-20,#		•
Missouri	•			•-12	•-17,#								•
Montana	•-4		•	•-13		•						•	
Nebraska	•			•-12	•-16	•							
Nevada	•	•-j	•-11	•-13	•-19	•	•			•			•
New Hampshire	•-4	•-j	•	•-12	•-17	•	•	•-#		•	•-#		•
New Jersey	•-1	•-j	•	•-12	•-19	•							
New Mexico	•-1,4	•-j	•	•-13	•-17	•	•						•-25
New York	•-1	•	•	•-13	•-17	•			•-n	•-a,#	•-20,f	•	•
North Carolina	•		•	•-12		•	•				•-20	•	•
North Dakota	•-1,4		•	•-13	•-17	•	•				•		
Ohio	•-4,8	•-j	•	•-12	•-17	•	•		•-n,o				•-25
Oklahoma	•-4	•-j	•-11	•-13	•-15	•	•				•-20	•	•
Oregon	•		•	•-12	•-19	•	•			•-b		•	•-25
Pennsylvania	•	•	•-d,#	•-13	•-19	•	•	•	•-9		•-#		•
Rhode Island	•-5	•	•	•-12	•-17	•	•	•	•		•-20,a		•
South Carolina	•-1,6	•-6,j	•	•-13	•-17	•	•					•	
South Dakota	•-4	•-j	•	•-12	•-19	•	•						
Tennessee	•	•-j	•	•-12	•-17	•	•					•	
Texas	•		•	•-13	•-17,#	•							•
Utah	•-4		•	•-12	•-19	•	•	•-#			•-22		•
Vermont	•-1	•-j	•	•	•-17	•	•						•
Virginia	•	•-j	•	•-13,c	•-17	•	•		•-n,o				•
Washington	•	•-j	•-11	•-13,a	•-17	•	•		•-o			•	•-25
West Virginia	•	•	•	•-12	•-17	•	•					•	•
Wisconsin	•-4,m	•-k	•	•-12	•-18	•	•				•	•	•-25
Wyoming	•-4		•	•-12	•-19	•	•					•	

Many state inspection regulations require that any equipment installed on a motorcycle must function properly even though the equipment is not required by law. Although this chart represents information from the most authoritative sources available as of the date shown above, the Motorcycle Industry council is not responsible for accuracy or completeness. Information concerning equipment requirements in Canada can be obtained from the Motorcycle & Moped Industry Council (MMIC) at 7181 Woodbine Ave., Suite 229A, Markham, Ontario, Canada L3R 1A3; (416) 470-6123.

Motorcycle Organizations

For a free catalog of MSF and *RiderCourse* publications and accessories, please call the Communications Department at (714) 727-3227, or write:

- Motorcycle Safety Foundation
  2 Jenner Street, Suite 150
  Irvine, California 92718-3812
  To find a *Motorcycle RiderCourse* near you:
  1-800-447-4700 (toll-free)

If you have questions concerning legislative matters, contact:

- Motorcycle Safety Foundation
  Government Relations/
      Eastern Resource Office
  1235 Jefferson Davis Highway, Suite 600
  Arlington, Virginia 22202
  (703) 521-0444

- American Motorcyclist Association
  P.O. Box 6114
  Westerville, Ohio 43081
  (614) 891-2425
  Information on becoming an AMA member:
  1-800-AMA-JOIN (toll-free)

- Discover Today's Motorcycling
  To learn more about buying a motorcycle, preparing to ride, how to finance, and how to get insured, get the *Straight Facts* brochures by calling at 1-800-833-3995. You will also be told how to find a *Motorcycle RiderCourse* near you.

- ATV Safety Institute
  2 Jenner Street, Suite 150
  Irvine, California 92718-3812
  (714) 727-3227
  To find an *ATV RiderCourse* or off-highway motorcycle course near you: 1-800-887-2887 (toll-free)

Photo/Illustration/Sidebar Credits

Photos

AGV USA Corp.: 47, 48
American Suzuki Motor Corp.: 17
Arai Helmet Ltd.: 45
BMW of North America, Inc.: 16, 22, 149
Rich Chenet/Courtesy of American Suzuki Motor Corp.: 15
Rich Cox/Slide Action: 16, 100
Firstgear/Intersport Fashions West: 51
Hein Gericke/Intersport Fashions West: 48, 50
Kawasaki Motors Corporation, USA: 18, 127
Nate Rauba: 18, 23, 26, 43, 45, 91, 97, 128, 143, 150–157
Sidi/Acerbis USA: 46
Yamaha Motor Corporation, USA: 17

Illustrations

Hector Cademartori: Front Cover, Back Cover, 10, 20, 28, 31, 32, 38, 52, 60, 74, 86, 98
Robert Enriquez/Robert Enriquez Illustration: 63, 66, 71, 81, 82, 83, 88, 89
JoAnne Meeker/The Creative Line: 69, 70, 75, 76, 77, 78, 79, 80, 81, 82, 83

Sidebars

The Un-Rider: Stuart Munro, p. 28
Checking Out: Gerald Lotto, p. 31
Mental Systems: William Cosby, p. 62
Looking In All Directions: Peter Fassnacht and William Cosby, p. 73
Riding At Night: David L. Hough, p. 93
Raising A Fallen Bike: David L. Hough, p. 96

Glossary

BAC – An abbreviation for Blood-Alcohol Concentration. BAC expresses the amount of alcohol in the body as a percentage of the body's total fluid.

Center of gravity – The point in an object where the force of gravity appears to act. If an object is balanced at any point on the vertical line passing through its center of gravity it will remain balanced.

Contact patch – Portion of a tire that is in contact with the road surface.

Convex mirrors – A mirror with an outward-curved surface. This type of mirror shows more area than a flat mirror, but objects appear farther away than they really are.

Coefficient of friction – The ratio of potential friction between two surfaces to the force pressing them together.

Counterbalancing – Adjusting body position and weight to balance a motorcycle at very low speeds. Requires weight shift counter, or opposite, to the lean of the motorcycle.

Countersteer – The initial steering input required to make a motorcycle lean to turn. Usually best described as push left—go left, push right—go right.

Counterweighting – Same as counterbalancing. Can be interchanged at will.

Decreasing-radius turn – A turn that becomes tighter.

Engine braking – Braking force created by the engine.

Following distance – Distance that you follow other vehicles, based on time and speed. The minimum distance at low speeds is two seconds.

Friction zone – Area of clutch-lever travel where the clutch starts to transmit power to the rear wheel.

Fuel-supply valve – Valve, usually on the left side of the engine, that controls the flow of gasoline. Typical positions are ON, OFF, RESERVE, and PRIME.

Headlight modulator – Electronic device that pulses the headlight, ideally to make the motorcycle more visible during the day. May not be legal in some states.

High-crowned road – Usually found on a rural roadway. Road surface arcs with high center and low sides. Permits road drainage. Can cause clearance problems when cornering.

High-side crash – When a motorcycle is leaning, the side closest to the road surface is called the "low side"; the other side is the "high side." A high-side crash is one in which the rider goes over the motorcycle's high side.

Impending skid – Used to describe a wheel at traction limit prior to loss of traction. Usually used in discussing maximum braking.

Lean angle – Degree that the motorcycle is leaned during a turn. The turning happens as a result of the lean angle.

Load triangle – Triangle formed by the lines from the rider's head to the front and rear axles, and the line between the two axles. When loading a motorcycle, heavier items should be placed within or as close to this triangle as possible.

Low-side crash – Crash in which the rider goes over the motorcycle's low side. (See high-side crash.)

Maximum load capacity – Difference between the empty weight and the maximum allowable weight of the motorcycle and all of its load, including the rider and passenger. Specified by the manufacturer.

The total weight of the motorcycle and load is called GVWR (gross vehicle weight rating).

Maximum braking – The full application of both brakes at impending skid to achieve minimum stopping distance.

Off-camber turn – Corner in which the road surface slopes down to the outside of the turn.

Path of travel – Where the motorcycle will go.

Petcock – Variation of term: fuel-supply valve.

Range – A term used to describe the practice riding facility. Typically a large, paved parking area where riding skill exercises are conducted.

Reaction time – Interval between when a rider perceives a new situation and takes action. Normally around 0.75 seconds.

RiderCourse – Rider-training class developed by the Motorcycle Safety Foundation. There are two versions, the *Motorcycle RiderCourse: Riding and Street Skills* (aimed at beginning riders) and the *Experience RiderCourse* (which helps veteran riders fine-tune their skills).

Retroreflective – The reflection of light rays parallel to their source.

Rolling moment – A technical term used to describe the inertial forces that operate about the axis of rotation while a motorcycle is leaning or "rolling."

SIPDE – Mental process used to make judgments and take action in traffic. Stands for **S**can, **I**dentify, **P**redict, **D**ecide, **E**xecute.

Simple reaction time – Interval between when a rider decides what to do and when he actually begins doing it. Normally around 0.5 seconds.

Single-track vehicle – An engineering term used to describe motorcycles, bicycles and other two-wheelers with one wheel in front of the other. Single-track vehicles must lean to turn.

Skid – (Also called slide.) Movement that occurs when a tire loses its grip on the road and slides, either along or across the surface.

Space cushion – Area you can create and maintain between yourself and other vehicles. Allows time for reacting to changing situations and leaves an alternative path of travel.

Staggered formation – Group riding formation in which the leader rides in the left portion of lane and the next rider to the right, one second behind. Following riders continue this pattern while maintaining a two-second following distance from the rider directly ahead.

T-CLOCK – Simple term used to remember motorcycle components that should be examined during a pre-ride inspection. The components are: **T**ires and wheels; **C**ontrols, such as levers, cables, and throttle; **L**ights and electrics; **O**ils and lubricants; **C**hassis and chain; and **K**ickstand.

Target fixation – Staring at an area or object to such an extent that it draws you to it.

Traction – Friction between tires and the road surface.

Tubeless tires – Tubeless tires, like those on most modern street motorcycles, run cooler because tire tube friction is eliminated and heat retaining mass is reduced. Unsprung weight is also reduced.

Unified or integrated braking system – This system links front and rear brake operation. A portion of the rear-brake pressure is applied to one of the front brakes when the rear brake pedal is applied.

Vacuum fuel-supply valve – A device that uses the vacuum created by a running engine to open a diaphragm-controlled fuel-supply valve. Automatically shuts off fuel supply when engine stops.

Weave – Oscillation of the rear tire.

Wheel lock-up – Condition where brakes cause a wheel to stop turning, even though the machine is still moving. It occurs when the braking effort is greater than the available friction between tire and road surface. The tire slides instead of gripping the surface.

Wobble – Rapid shaking of the handlebar.

Index

Answers to Self-Tests

Chapter 1: The Challenge of Motorcycling
1—c; 2—b; 3—d; 4—d

Chapter 2: Basic Riding Skills
1—a; 2—c; 3—Slow, Look, Lean, Roll (on the throttle); 4—d

Chapter 3: Mental Preparation
1—d; 2—b; 3—90%; 4—Anger, grief

Chapter 4: Riding Straight
1—False; 2—True; 3—False; 4—True

Chapter 5: Protective Riding Gear
1—Comfort, protection; 2—d; 3—b; 4—d

Chapter 6: Motorcycle Inspection, Care, and Troubleshooting
1—Tires & wheels, Controls, Lights & electrics, Oils & fluids, Chassis & chain, Kickstand; 2—False; 3—True; 4—True

Chapter 7: Street Strategies and the Visual Edge
1—c; 2—d; 3—a; 4—d; 5—b

Chapter 9: Special Situations
1—d; 2—b; 3—a; 4—c

Chapter 10: Group Riding
1—b; 2—c; 3—b; 4—False

Chapter 11: Traction
1—False; 2—True; 3—True; 4—False

Chapter 12: The Traction-Pie Analogy
1—b; 2—False; 3—c; 4—False

Chapter 13: Countersteering
1—b; 2—b; 3—c; 4—b

Chapter 14: Cornering
1—Path (or line) and speed; 2—b; 3—c; 4—True; 5—a

Chapter 15: Low- and High-Speed Turning
1—c; 2—a; 3—d; 4—False

Chapter 16: Off-Highway Riding
1—False; 2—True; 3—False; 4—True